TWO PLAYS

PLAYS BY PETER WEISS

Two Plays   1970
The Investigation   1966
The Persecution and Assassination of Jean-Paul Marat as Performed by the Inmates of the Asylum of Charenton under the Direction of the Marquis de Sade   1965

TWO PLAYS

BY PETER WEISS

Song of the Lusitanian Bogey

TRANSLATED BY LEE BAXANDALL

*Discourse on the Progress of the
Prolonged War of Liberation in Viet Nam
and the Events Leading Up to It
as Illustration of the Necessity for
Armed Resistance Against Oppression
and on the Attempts of the
United States of America to Destroy
the Foundations of Revolution*

TRANSLATED BY GEOFFREY SKELTON

ATHENEUM *New York* **1970**

CONTENTS

Song of the Lusitanian Bogey   1

    ACT ONE   5

    ACT TWO   34

Discourse on . . . Viet Nam   65

    PART ONE   70

    PART TWO   148

    CHRONOLOGY   230

Song of the Lusitanian Bogey

7 players, 4 female, 3 male, represent all of the roles in the play. Wearing their everyday clothing. Transitions from one role to another can be indicated by the simplest means. A single object will do it: a sun helmet, a crucifix, a bishop's hat, a stick, a sack, etc. In a very few cases a half mask. The characterizations should not be artfully contrived. The means of their making should be transparent. That is, the effect should be one of street-corner improvisations. In no case may showing the change from a European to an African role, and the reverse, depend on make-up and masking. Whatever the color of their skin, the actors speak interchangeably for Europeans and Africans. Only by the mode of their acting do they take a position on the conflicts.

A couple of crude board walls may define the stage space. On stage right the figure of THE BOGEY is located. It should be larger than life, and menacing. It may be constructed of scrap iron. Over the face, a flap, which may be lifted from the back. In the opening appears the face of the player who assumes the speeches of THE BOGEY at a given moment. The flap must be made to drop shut with a crash. The construction of THE BOGEY must be such that the figure may fall over on hinges at the play's end.

3 or 4 musicians support the players. If possible they should be visible at the side of the stage. It is advantageous if at times they move onto the stage with the players. Their instruments are, for example, a mouth harmonica, an accordion, a guitar, a flute, a hand drum.

The lighting continually bright.

FEMALE ACTORS

1

2

3

4

MALE ACTORS

5
6
7

Neither this distribution of the ensemble nor this number of actors is obligatory. Changes may be made, suited to the possibilities of the theater or the intentions of the director.

The performance directions grew out of rehearsal work for the premiere of the play at the Scala Theater of Stockholm.

Gunilla Palmstierna-Weiss designed the stage and the costumes.

Etienne Glaser directed the theater collective, in which everyone, together with the author, lent a hand in shaping the performance style.

The music for the play was written by Bengt Arne Wallin.

The premiere took place January 20, 1967.

The actors:

Lena Brundin, Monica Nielsen, Yvonne Lundeqvist, Isa Quensel, Allan Edwall, Nils Eklund, Björn Gustafson.

Translator's note:

The American premiere took place on January 2, 1968, at the St. Marks Playhouse, New York City.

The play was the first presentation of the Negro Ensemble Company, a project codirected by Douglas Turner Ward, Robert Hooks and Gerald S. Krone.

Production director was Michael A. Schultz. The dance director was Louis Johnson. The sets were designed by Edward Burbridge, the costumes by Bernard Johnson.

A new musical score was composed by Coleridge-Taylor Perkinson.

The number of performers was increased to nine. They were: Rosalind Cash, David Downing, Arthur French, Moses Gunn, William Jay, Judyann Jonsson, Denise Nicholas, Hattie Winston and Allie Woods.

ACT ONE

SCENE I

[*Entrance of the actresses and actors. 1 and 7 carry on sticks a small curtain of shabby red velvet. 5 goes behind the curtain. The other actresses and actors gather around* THE BOGEY. *On stage left, 5 steps from behind the curtain. He wears a tail coat, a cylinder hat and a broad honorary ribbon.*]

5: Fear and outrage rape and knife
   are a BOGEY's staff of life
   Though his essence is trickery
   what's inside is not hard to see
   Tin and nightsticks rags and straw
   make the substance of his law
        [*2, 3 and 4 hang some objects on* THE BOGEY
        which will be used later in the play.]

5: Cunning gall deceit and lying
   the Spirit wants and we're supplying
   Sell-out hatred stink of urine
   we're his voice and do his lurin'
   Incense poison churchly bells
   make you forget the Specter smells
        [*6 behind* THE BOGEY *shakes the figure. The
        tin rattles.*]

5: Examine close this lump of lead
   rust and bumps about his head
   See the mouth with sharp teeth gleaming
   set to yawn and fit for screaming
   On the skull of tin will ride
   a hat of dignity—his pride
        [*6 demonstratively clangs the tin. 5 tosses the*

cylinder hat to 2, which she balances on THE
BOGEY. *4 hangs a sack around* THE BOGEY.]

5: Coal sacks thrown across his chest
fit him out with tails and vest
Add a ribbon of renown
master of the land and town
Last of all a crucifix
without this he'd just be nix

> [*5 tosses the honorary ribbon to 3, and she at-
> taches it to* THE BOGEY. *5 pulls a crucifix out of
> his pocket, throws it to 4. She hangs it on* THE
> BOGEY.*]

5: If our skeletal machine
shakes and wobbles something mean
Still it's very like that One
with whom we're sadly not yet done
All of us know his true name
you will recognize his game

> [*5 takes himself off behind the curtain. The
> curtain is carried away. The face of* THE BOGEY
> *clangs open. 6 behind* THE BOGEY. *The mouth
> stretches into a big yawn.*]

BOGEY: I receive my injunctions
from the Lord God
It is Lusitania's task
to disseminate the Holy Gospel
on the earth
Repeatedly it is shown in history
that man is not capable
of guiding himself
He needs the direction of an authority
which will save him
from sinking down
into self-interest and materialism
The competition for economic gain
and a raise in the standard of living
causes the true spirit of mankind to be forgotten

and an era of soullessness
and of emptiness
is begotten
My purpose it must be
to rescue mankind
from the temptations of that abyss and
to train him
to be an ethical being
always conscious
of the other and higher world
which exists
on the far side of this
the fleeting world
of technology
    [*Yawns.*]

1: We give in almost to the temptation to say
that good things will come to those who long
    suffer and pray
But if we look around the shock will enrage us
everywhere the agents and the small deaths of
    wages
Eliminating opponents is the basic condition
what else could you expect with such a system

Absolutely needed by the man
is the ignorance of all who under him stand
So many as possible should neither read nor
    write
misunderstandings cannot therefore come to light
And while they drudge for bare survival's
    pittance
they have not strength to rise against him in
    quittance

This all makes greatest sense to the man's
    landlords
for from this system come their great rewards

And so long as no reversals make his generals
    doubt
and while capital finds a favorable opening about
The cream of society will pledge him its trust
he alone shall keep watch on its doings and
    thrust
            [*7 enters with a General's hat and shoulder
            decorations. Smart military movements.*]
7: A productive society
is based on hard and
self-sacrificing work
Each person is dutybound to do
his damnedest just there
where he now stands
on the basis of his ethical
cultural and financial
footing
A healthy society functions
by virtue of the services
which the classes do
each for the others

Our basic ideas are
God patriotism and family
            [*2, 3, 4, 5, 6 as* CHORUS.]
CHORUS: God patriotism and family
        7: Lusitania reaches over the seas
Lusitania is united and forever
CHORUS: Lusitania is united and forever
        2: A delegation from Alentejo
begs most humbly
permission to kiss
Your Excellency's hand
            [*6 holds out an elongated hand from* THE
            BOGEY. *3, 4 sink to their knees before the
            hand and kiss it.*]

1: So he and those with him rule throughout our
   land
   and it seems that they've still got it firmly in
   hand
   Rebels are found out wherever they may operate
   and are tossed into cells till they learn to
   cooperate

   His experts who are with the secret police agency
   use the newest and best torture in each
   contingency
   Making sure that their real power will be
   indicated
   prisoners are lined up before the wall and
   liquidated

   Still it must be admitted that lately
   the signs of unrest have grown greatly
   Even many who can neither read nor write
   have started to see things in a new light
        [6 *opens the face of* THE BOGEY *with a clatter.*
        6 *yells loudly.*]

BOGEY: Barbarism
   is threatening the world
   The enemy
   is advancing in our land
   Spreading poisonous
   internationalism
   Putting in danger
   the sacred rights of property
   Undermining
   family morality
   Eroding
   our previous religion—
        [*Yawns.*]
   The young

as never before
you must become strong
in body and in spirit
so that tomorrow
we are prepared
to assign the soldiers for
the defense of our values

> [6 *delivers the last sentence of* THE BOGEY's
> *speech as an aria. 2, 3, 4, 5 represent a jubilant
> and obedient crowd. Immediately thereafter 3
> and 7 bend down. 5 leaps upon their backs.*]

5: We have to make it our duty
to see that our way of life
is preserved
for it displays everywhere
our great historical
accomplishments
We must have
a steady standing reserve
to our labor force
which carries out all those jobs
for which we were
not born
I have always said
that a country's civilization
may be judged by the number of
its serving personnel
Wherever the servantry has vanished
civilization has vanished

> [3 *and 7 come forward during this speech, bent
> beneath their load. 6, as servant, accompanies
> the group, pantomiming a variety of atten-
> tions.*]

5: Naturally since I take a liberal stand
I favor self-improvement for any man
Juana the newspaper

> [5 *claps his hands. 4 springs over to him. 1 claps*

her hands, 4 hurries a few times between 1
and 5.]

1: Hired help have rights which may be defined
as a modern woman I keep it in mind
Juana brush my hair
      [5 down with the help of 6. 7, on his knees, of-
      fers an easy chair for 5. 3 represents the chair
      back. 5 settles himself comfortably.]

4: Up since 5 A.M. today
my job of work goes this way
Dust the house and scrub the floor
Take the breakfast to their door
Wash up the service and run to the baker
then to the tinsmith and the shoemaker
Empty chamberpots and make the beds
Brush master's suits for any loose threads
Sew on buttons and wash the clothing
then for the wine and the meat I'm going
Cook the lunch and the table lay
Balance the soup upon a tray
Apron and cap without a spot
Bring in the wine and the coffee pot
Wash up the service and mend the clothes
by mistake taking a brief doze
Rake the lawn and check each dish
Quickly then to the market for fish
Peel the potatoes and the fish fileted
and the master's come home he's not delayed
Attend at the dinner and clear the service
without a racket that could make him nervous
Wash everything up and spend the evening
at the job of silver cleaning
Then up I go to fetch their shoes
this I do quietly while they snooze
And if the master doesn't want a late bite
I'll get to bed round about midnight

1: I think our Juana has a very nice sleeping space

and had she not well it would be quite a disgrace

4: It may not be much larger than a coffin
   but I've given my thanks for it very often

1: Our Juana knows perfectly her probable fate
   had we not taken her up to live within our gate

5: And our Juana boastfully can say
   200 escudos are her monthly pay

4: Not a bit of it can I save yet I cannot shirk
   from adding I rejoice to have regular work

1: It's gotten so anything turns these people's heads
     around
   nowadays every sort of propaganda is found
         [6 *appears behind* THE BOGEY. *In a whining voice.*]

BOGEY: The conspiracies
       of our enemies
       are aimed especially to
       the overseas provinces
       to our black fellow citizens
       In view of their lack of maturity
       their childlike backwardness
       they are wide open
       to the efforts of these elements
       to incite them
       having as their purpose
       the destruction
       of our ideals
         [6 *leans sideways and forward from behind*
         THE BOGEY. *Grasps the crucifix. Preaching in
         a changed voice.*]

6: The Vicar of God in this world
   looks to Portugal with confidence
   The Holy Father
   sends his salutations to Portugal
         [7 *has put on the General's hat again.*]

7: Followed with the blessings of their mothers
   the youth of Portugal hurry

to the defense of the Overseas Provinces
[*6 with again the voice of* THE BOGEY.]
6: To offer a paternal hand to these
endangered ones
to defend and give guidance to them
that is our Civilizing mission

SCENE II

[*4 solemnly, with a big voice. 3 and 7 in devotional
postures.*]
4: The mission of Civilizing
springs from the principle
of a Christian love of neighbor
By the strength of our open outlook
we shall forge a harmony
between the Exotic
and the Occident
[*3, 4, 7 as* CHORUS.]
CHORUS: In the Overseas Provinces
which have belonged to us
for 500 years
3: Genuine harmony is based
on the kinship of soul with soul
Only thus may we conceive
authentic solidarity
All men have their beginning in God
and division there can never be
between the black and white
CHORUS: In the Overseas Provinces
which have belonged to us
for 500 years
7: Yet though all men before God stand equal
no obligation on us follows
to hand over rights to the underdeveloped
who truth to tell are not up to them

They are yet by far too distant
from the social-cultural qualifications
that we expect and rightly
CHORUS: In the Overseas Provinces
which have belonged to us
for 500 years

> [1, 4 and 5 form a heroic tableau. 5 represents
> the explorer Diego Cao, 4 depicts the con-
> quered African population. The sack has been
> laid over 4. 1 puts a helmet on 5. Presses a
> sword into his raised hand. Turned about, the
> sword can become a cross.]

2: Diego Cao with his sailing fleet came
to the mouth of Congo's great brown stream
Found there a people of peaceable habits
free-born workers of land and hunters of the
forest
They already had tools made of iron and pots
made of copper
they worked up carpets carved in gold and ivory
had domesticized animals cattle in pastures
Diego Cao and his people were pleased with it
here where they were taken in and welcomed
and they made an exchange of gifts
then they erected near Cabinda
the first of their forts

Diego Cao next with all his people
traveled down the fertile coast
teaching the populace of the country
the Christian beliefs
He dispatched a shipload of natives
over the ocean to his homeland harbor
that all might see what he had found here
Diego Cao and his crew grew more and more
delighted with it
here where they were taken in and welcomed

but no longer were they grateful for gifts
then they erected by Luanda
the second of their forts

Diego Cao sailed with all his vessels
up the swollen Cuanza toward its source
Claiming the rosewood and mahogany as his own
as well as the metals and the precious stones
The inhabitants of the country
as well as spices fruits and exotic treasures
made up the cargoes of his caravels
Diego Cao and his men were the most pleased
    when they settled
upon the highlands of Benguela where they
no longer were taken in and welcomed
and they erected on the Kunene
the third of their forts
        [7 enters with a large Bishop's hat. 3 ceremoni-
        ously settles broad ribbons about his shoulders.]
7: Archbishop of the city of Luanda
on the fish-rich coast of the South Atlantic
I took a personal concern for
what was shipped from our possession
across the water to the other possessions
of the world kingdom of Lusitania
        [6 appears as a man-in-arms.]
6: Got another 100 workhands on board
young men and women
healthy children
That makes up the thousand scheduled
for this month
7: And have they all been baptized
6: They all are baptized
Your Holiness
7: Then have them look here
that I may bless them before departure
2: Diego Cao with his sailing fleet came

into the land between the Congo and the
        Kunene
And he took from the inhabitants their land
and he took from them all else belonging to
        them
And he stripped the villages of their occupants
so the villages turned to shambles and the fields
        lay fallow
Each single year he dragged off 10,000 captives
while those who came later shipped away millions
In this way Diego Cao taught
a people who received him kindly
to know a hatred
that ever since has burned

> [*During the last verse the group dissolves and
> moves slowly to exit. 7, as the Bishop, leads the
> group. 6 takes charge of actress 4 covered by
> the sack. Then immediately a regrouping for a
> new scene. 2 becomes the principal singer. The
> other actors and actresses form together into a*
> Chorus.]

Chorus: The earth it rips open it tears open it heaves
        open
     2: Let the men feel the pains of the women in
        labor
Chorus: The earth it rips open it tears open it heaves
        open
     2: Let the men feel the pains of giving birth
Chorus: The earth it rips open it tears open it heaves
        open
     2: Let the men feel the bloody giving of birth
Chorus: The earth it rips open it tears open it heaves
        open
     2: Let mankind be in labor and the fruit burst
        forth

> [*5 steps forward. 2 in collapse.*]

     5: From the study of history we will plainly learn

that the uprisings came by yearly turn
They discharged their spears and they hurled
    their darts
at an enemy heavily armed in all parts
When hunger and need had forced them to
    surrender
the best of them were no longer alive to
    remember
On every hand their rich complex traditions
were wiped out by invading penal expeditions
The families were dissolved and scattered the kin
so that no one would know who stood next to
    him
Here is the reason and it is stark
why the African continent is labeled Dark

[6 *appears behind* THE BOGEY. *In a shrill voice.*]

BOGEY: Those peoples of the bush
have no feeling for nationhood
It is we
who awaken in them the idea
of a community

5: The man they call Deceiver the last of Cao's
    descendants
speaks of Brotherhood and civilized
    interdependence
What is offered from Europe with all its
    achievement
should become local usage by all means and
    common agreement
That's what is written in The Deceiver's decree
which every literate person may go and see

BOGEY: Habits and customs
can only be granted recognition
when they are compatible
with the morals and foundation
of our human nature
as well as the

free exercise of Lusitanian
sovereignty

SCENE III

    5: How many are you
       in your country
          [2, 3, 4 *as* CHORUS.]
CHORUS: We are 5 million
       in our country
    5: How many Civilizers are
       in your country
CHORUS: 100,000 Civilizers are
       in our country
    5: 50 of you
       for each of the Civilizers
       in your country
          [6 *in* THE BOGEY *bends far forward. He shouts
          cadence for the March of the Colonizers. 1, 3,
          4, 7 begin to march. 2 and 5 join. All in*
          CHORUS.]
CHORUS: Yet it is we who are practical to Africa
       we who fight the sleeping sickness and malaria
       Who but we have unlocked the earth's own
          treasure
       so that many may enjoy it in some measure
       We are the ones who plant the highlands with
          wheat
       who harvest the rice and sesame seed
       who cultivate sugar coffee tobacco and cotton
       and ore manganese diamonds from the
          mountains have gotten
       We bring up the earth's oil and draw the salt
          from mines
       we build transport roads and lay down rail lines
       The savannas and rain forests we level

with our ships we have opened these seas to
    travel
All this with the help of monopoly and our
    corporations
bringing this land to the level of good
    Civilizations
    [With this concluded, a division into the fol-
    lowing groupings: 5 and 7 stand left. 1, 2, 3, 4
    stand right as the Chorus. *6 in the middle.]*

6: To the forests I have come
    to cut wood
5 AND 7: Cut the wood cut the wood
    in the rain forests
CHORUS: The forests are not ours
    Let us curse the forests
6: To the fields I have come
    to guard the cattle
5 AND 7: Guard the cattle guard the cattle
    of the fields
CHORUS: The fields are not ours
    Let us curse the fields
6: To the mountains I have come
    to hunt animals
5 AND 7: Drive the animals drive the animals
    before the guns
CHORUS: The mountains are not ours
    Let us curse the mountains
6: To the cities I have come
    to build myself a house
5 AND 7: Polish my boots nigger
    Carry my bag
CHORUS: The cities are not ours
    Let us curse the cities
7: We allow everyone the chance
    to seek the rights of citizenship
    Everyone who shows good will
    and learns and works well

        that person is on his way
        to integration
5:   I am what they call assimilated
        To be assimilated
        I have fulfilled the following conditions
        I have no previous record of convictions
        I fluently speak
        the language of the mother country
        Without difficulty I can write
        the language of the mother country
        I know the glorious history
        of the mother country
        I have made a declaration of loyalty
        I produced two witnesses
        to my personal character
        I have a certificate of health
        I have steady work
        I have a regular income
        I have always paid my taxes on time
        I go regularly to church service
        I have acquired the level of education
        and taken on the habits
        which are requisite
        for the granting of public
        and private rights
        Now I may take part
        in the voting
        Now I may join
        one of the unions which
        are established by the government
        I am one of 30,000 assimilated
        in Lusitania's province of Angola
        I am that one assimilated
        among 100 African workers
                [*All the other actors and actresses, except 4,
                move in a circle.*]

4: We are the 99 of 100
   African workers in Angola
   who never had the time
   nor had the means
   to learn to read and write
   We work from the age of 10 years
   until death
   which often greets us early
   We may not take part
   in the voting
   For us there are no unions
   We must carry out the work given us
   under the existing contract system
   which pays 7 dollars every month
        [*All actors and actresses in one row.*]

7: Those unsuited to be educated
   are taken on in public hire
   during only 6 months of the year

4, 5, 6: So that they don't loaf around
   murder and steal and leave themselves open
   to the urgings of foreign agents

2: The rest of the time they may
   farm upon their own land

3: If they have their own land
        [*1 and 7 go apart into the middle.*]

1: Here is a piece of land
   on the African continent
   Here we plant peanuts

5: How do you plant your peanuts

7: With a branch
   we dig a furrow
   in the dry earth

1: We bore the holes
   in the furrows
   with our toes

7: Into the holes

we put the seeds
1: Now we must wait
for the rain
that will grow peanuts for us
1 AND 7: On this piece of earth
out of 11⅔ million square miles
on the great African
continent

> [*2, 3, 4, 5, 6 conversing eagerly. They overlap
> each other's speeches and repeat the statements
> and questions in multiple echo.*]

If the native can get up the money
to obtain his own land
then he has to oblige himself
to farm the land according
to regulations

What are the regulations

He must farm the land as
the experts tell him to
And if he gets his qualification
with the designation Model J
then the land is his

How does he get his qualification

If he is a planter of coffee
he must raise 5,000 trees
A smaller number and he is
not yet an owner of land

And if he doesn't manage to
cultivate 5,000 trees

Then the land is
taken from him

And if he has managed with 5,000 trees
then may he remain upon his land

He may stay upon his land
6 months of the year
Then he too can be taken off elsewhere
if the needs of the labor force
require it

And when he gets back

By that time our own planters
will have taken over the planting
You understand it must be
because of the nation's economy
    [*Concluding with a general "Hey!" as after a
    successful circus act.*]

SCENE IV

[*In the row the performance of power is panto-
mimed.*]
5: We are having one terrific time
    getting the needed labor force together
4: On its own the human resource simply
    does not rise to the call
6: Recruiters have to run all over the landscape
    in order to get those people together
        [*6 pulls a billy-club from* THE BOGEY. *1, 2, 3, 4
        move left in flight. 6 stations himself center
        with the billy-club raised. 5 and 7 stand right.*]
5: The Chief of Post rules the village
    when a visit is made from outside
    and he draws out papers
    we know
    workers must be rounded up
    The Chief of Post takes out his billy-club
    The Chief of Post wishes to gain his head-price
    We run off into the bush

we keep ourselves hidden
and when we come back
we find the village empty
Our women taken away to work
in a far district
          [1, 2, 3, 4 *as* CHORUS.]
CHORUS: Driven by blows into the street
          Shown no place to sleep
          Lay by night under the open sky
          Our children cried with hunger
          They shook out a bag of cornmeal before us
          We called to them
          this is moldy cornmeal and full of worms
          With his billy-club the foreman hit us
                    [3 *standing without movement, hands behind*
                    her back. Softly singing.]
     3: Look at my hands my hands
          they were hit by the billy
                    [5 AND 7 *in canon.*]
          Hit this nigger with the billy
          Hit her hit her with the billy
     3: The foreman hit at my hands
          The foreman hits the women with the billy
5 AND 7: Hit her on the hands with the billy
          Hit her hit her with the billy
     3: The billy has a mouth
          The billy bites holes in my hands
          The billy bites holes
          in the hands of the women
     5: We must inspire the natives with
          the idea of work
          We must bring them around to see
          that the only way they can improve
          their social condition
          is work
     7: They do not have the gift for logical thinking
          They are unable to plan

All that they can see is today
They do not think for tomorrow
Without us
they would collapse into
indifference

5: Not long ago I watched a nigger
She had 2 children that had died
Cry she did not
The next day she worked
as always
Forgotten were those
children
          [*3 steps forward.*]

3: 14 hours in a day
I worked on the cotton plantation
My eldest daughter
last I heard was down at the port Benguela
I've had no news of her
in a year now
My sons are
supposed to be in Mossamedes
at the fish-meal factory
They're 12 and 15 years of age
My husband was
transported half a year ago
Sent to Malanje
to the asbestos pits
Don't know
if he is still there
Have only my
daughter 7 years old with me
Helps me with the picking
Out of my 200 escudos this month
Following deductions I've got
150 escudos
Cornmeal 5 escudos for 2 pounds
Beans 3 escudos for 2 pounds

Dried fish 5 escudos for 2 pounds
Palm oil 9 escudos for a quart
Really did need a dress
A yard of cotton 20 escudos
Have to forget about the dress
Will my husband locate me
when he comes back
Will my sons be able to find me
They don't know
that I am at the cotton plantation
nobody left at the village
who will know us

> [*The following scene may be performed as a
> shadow play. 3 and 5 move swiftly to hold
> stretched a piece of material fastened to two
> staves. 6 and 7 stand behind the cloth. The ma-
> terial has a strong light on it from the rear. In
> rapid sequence 6 and 7 alter their postures and
> express the situations by images. In the shadow
> play 3 and 5 speak on behalf of the figures be-
> hind the cloth. They quote.*]

7: Ask all around the plantations
for my wife
for my children
nobody has seen them
3: Show us your work pass
7: Here is my work pass
3: You were in Malanje
7: I was in Malanje
in the asbestos pits
3: There is no stamp for the recent weeks
That's punishable
7: Had no time
to go for the stamp
Looked for my wife
for my children
3: Show your money

7: Haven't any more money
What was left from my pay
went for the train trip

3: Knocking about without money
That's punishable

7: Wanted to work at home
with my wife
with my children

3: There's no permission stamp for taking residence
in this district
That's punishable

7: Had no time
to go for a residence permit
Looking for my wife
for my children

3: Don't you know
that you're in for penal labor
when your passbook's not in order

7: But I just put in 6 months
in the pits of Malanje

3: Since you're straying around
without a permanent residence
and since you haven't any work
and no money
you'll now be taken to a camp
where they'll teach you
to live up to
your legal obligations

> [*End of the shadow play. The cloth is quickly
> cleared. 6 gives 7 a shove forward.*]

6: So that the dangers of anarchy will be defeated
we have to keep an eye
systematically on the natives
Each able-bodied one gets a passbook
Each time he's employed it's entered in
and all his official data is shown
If the native doesn't know

enough to carry his book
he must be sent for a year
into a camp for those who don't easily learn
to work without wages
2: Run Antelope-Man run
The hunter's coming with the hounds

Run fast from the hounds
Antelope-Man

Run Rabbit-Man run
The hunter's coming with his gun

Hide yourself from the hunter
Rabbit-Man

Run Fieldmouse-Man run
The hunter's shooting at you

Burrow away from the bullets
Fieldmouse-Man
Burrow away in the earth

SCENE V

5: The earlier slave-retainer took an interest
in keeping well and strong and active all his men
As for his horse and oxen so he cared about his
        men
Today it isn't that he buys his native
he gets him on consignment from the
        government
If he should come down sick or die
it's no concern of his
Another hand will take the place
        [1, 2, 3, 4, 7 *form together as a* CHORUS.]

CHORUS: The workers who are white men in our land
        get 6 times higher pay put into their hand
        than in a month we're paid for longer hours
        and the taxes on their pay are less than ours

        The workers who are white men in our land
        wish with the law and the power to find their
            stand
        And though many of them also neither read nor
            write
        they set themselves apart from us for they're
            white

        The workers who are white men in our land
        refuse to stick by us in a common stand
        They see our place as far beneath their level
        Will we not serve they kick the common devil

        The workers who are white men in our land
        won't comprehend or simply can't
        who it is that makes us devils in their eye
        and who it is that gains the most thereby
            [6 yelling from THE BOGEY.]
BOGEY: Within a world
        where people don't know the meaning of dignity
        where loyalty and respect
        scarcely exist between men
        where prejudice and dissension
        are on the rise
        Lusitania
        holds to its course—
            [Yawns.]
        There are those who say
        the problems of the State
        ought to be solved
        in a democratic way
        that meaning

as many as possible
should govern
We however have the courage to say
that in such manner
no just peaceful and
progressive solution
may be reached
Therefore exactly as we are opponents of
Syndicalism Liberalism
Parliamentarism Socialism
and every kind of
Bolshevism
so too are we against
Democracy
Within a world
which is threatened by Vandals
we are realizing the principle
of a State leadership
by the Elite
> [*1 steps to center of stage. Before her 5. 7 to
> the side. Gathered on left 2, 3, and 4.*]

1: My name is Anna and I'm in service
in a household at Nova Lisboa
Living with my family on the edge of the city
I get up before sunrise
I fix the cornmush for my children
I go the long way to my work on foot
I'm pregnant in the sixth month
Now after 12 hours of service I want
to go home

5: Here are more shirts to be ironed

1: I have to go home now
One of my children has fever
It must be taken to the mission hospital
> [*6 steps forward as Policeman.*]

5: This girl here dares to speak back to me
> [*6 pantomimes the actions.*]

6: I take the girl off
She defends herself
And she gets her answer
She wants to tear free
For that she gets a foot in the stomach
    [*1 collapses. 7 steps forward.*]
7: I'm the husband of Anna
Anna hasn't come home
Every other day she
comes back after sundown
5: Anna went home as always
7: Policeman sir
Anna hasn't come home
Every other day she
comes back after sundown
6: I know nothing about your Anna
    [*2, 3, 4 step forward as* Chorus. *5, 6, 7 step*
    back. 1 alone in the middle of stage. Chorus
    behind her in a tight row.]
Chorus: Where have they taken you
Anna
1: I'm lying on a clay floor
in a room
Chorus: What kind of a room
Anna
1: The window has bars
the door is locked shut
Chorus: Do you still have your headscarf
Anna
1: No
I don't have a headscarf
Chorus: Do you still have your shoes
Anna
1: No
I don't have any shoes
Chorus: Are you still in your dress
Anna

      1: No
        I don't have a dress
CHORUS: Are you still carrying a child
        Anna
      1: No
        I'm not carrying a child
CHORUS: How can we be of help
        Anna
      1: Tell my husband
        where I am
CHORUS: What does your house look like
        Anna
        Describe it to us
        so we can find it
        so we can bring news of you
        to your husband
        your children
      1: The house is of old scrap metal
        in the settlement quarter
        on the edge of Nova Lisboa
CHORUS: How is it arranged
        Anna
        Describe it to us
        so we will know when we look in
        that it is your house
      1: There's a curtain made of sacks
        Cooking area on the right
        On the left the mat
        where we sleep
CHORUS: What else is there
        Anna
        Describe it to us
        so we will be sure when we look around
        that it is your house
      1: There's a trunk on which we eat
        There's a cooking pot
        There's a pail

You'll see flies on the pail
The flies fly from the pail
over to the children
The flies settle
on the eyes of the children
One of my children has fever

CHORUS: Is there nothing else in your house
Anna
except for the curtain made of sacks
except for the cooking area the pot and the trunk
except for the mat and the pail with the flies

1: No
that is all

CHORUS: We will try
Anna
to find your house among the other houses
on the edge of Nova Lisboa
and to bring
news of you
to your husband your children

ACT TWO

SCENE VI

[*5 and 7 on the left as Policemen. 6 enters.*]
6: Wow
    so that's Nova Lisboa
    Did you ever see so many houses
    Houses growing up to the sky
    Did you ever see such streets
    Smooth as a mirror and with trees planted
    Did you ever see such springs
    The water comes out of stone mouths
    I can go wash up there
        [*5 strolls past 6.*]
5: You get away from that
6: Wow
    what sort of a garden is this
    Did ever you see such blossoms
    and such green grass
    I can lie down in the shade there
        [*4 out of sight.*]
4: Don't gawk at things
        [*6 before* The Bogey. *The face visor stands
        open. 3 behind it with a feather duster.*]
6: Wow
    what sort of house is this
    with columns and a flag
3: The Governor lives here
6: He must be a great man
    to need such a great house.
        [*3 slams the visor shut. 6 to the front.*]
6: Well

what sort of house is this
with glass doors and gold design
5: That is a bank
6: Wow
What do they do here
5: That's were they handle the money
6: Well
let me in there
I'd like to handle a little money too
5: Watch out that you don't get locked up
[*6 at left, toward 7, who has put on the General's hat.*]
6: Wow
what sort of house is this
with so many windows and a
General in front of a turning door
7: That is a hotel
6: I'd like to live in a hotel too
7: Beat it
[*6 enterprisingly goes up to 7. 7 moves as
though to strike him, and 6 retreats. Flees.
Runs to 5. 5 offers to strike him. 6 hurries back.
7 at him. Again a blow. 6 falls. Lies without
moving. 5 lays the sack over him. 5 goes back to
the right.*]
5: Racial discrimination does not exist here
Distinctions are strictly of a social nature
Blacks are simply not upon the level
to go into the bars or tennis club
[*7 goes back to left.*]
7: We put no barriers to the choices of vocation
In theory all careers are open to the assimilated
But as it turns out they're menials mainly
For the higher posts to speak frankly
Blacks aren't competent
[*1, 2, 4 come forward as* CHORUS.]
CHORUS: None the less with relentless

Civilizing patience we slowly
guide the people from the darkness
where long ago
we discovered them
        [*6 throws aside the sack. Stands up.*]
6: Wow
    I'd like a room
    I'd like to have my highest expectations fulfilled
    I'd like to have myself carried to bed for a siesta
    I'd like a refreshing bath in a sky-blue reservoir
    and hunt lions in the hunter's paradise
    Well
    I'd like to pay a visit to the
    picturesque waterfalls and the grottoes
    I'd like to inspect the ancient forests
    and the majestic mountains
    Wow
    I'd never like to forget
    these landscapes of
    an incomparable beauty
        [*6 goes slowly off at rear.*]
3: Following 500 years of a Civilizing Mission
    out of 100 Africans not more than one
    has his necessary reading and writing mastered
    for there is small chance of school for the poor
        bastard
    Of one and a half million school-age children
        this year
    at most about 90,000 are able to appear
    for study of the missionaries' catechism
    which is itself you might say a cataclysm
    Otherwise on the plantations there are some
        basic schools
    where above all the instruction must accord with
        the farming work rules
    Of the 12,000 who attend the primary level
    a couple of thousand each one a lucky devil

after exams can try for the high-school grades
be assimilated to avoid becoming lackeys and
     maids
Of those accepted 100 or near
will try to enter the universities this year
and of them perhaps two will succeed
in becoming academically degreed
After 500 years this much is real
as a result of relentless Civilizing zeal
     [1, 2, 4, 5, 6 *as* CHORUS.]
CHORUS: One and a half million young inhabitants
Of their own country
Future planners land-tillers city-builders
Doctors scientists poets
A mighty force of
Dammed-up talent
One and a half million cheap
new hands for labor
A mighty force of
Talent never employed
     [CHORUS *dissolves. 1, 2, 3, 4, 5, 6 form a group*
     on the left. 7 is to the right.]
5: We
residents of the province of Cabinda
most humbly beg the local authorities
for permission
to set up self-government
so we can regulate
our own concerns
7: What do you have to regulate
that we don't regulate
4: We'd like to send our children to school
6: We've put school money together for all of them
3: There is a school in the vicinity of our
     settlement
but the plantation owners protested
when we came with our children

5: For now there would have been many more
    black
children in the school than white

1: We want to set up our very own school
the other public school is
much too far from our village

7: If that's how it is all the fathers
who want this must write
their names on a petition

> [*5 goes to 7. Pantomimes the handing over of a
> written plea. 7 goes behind* THE BOGEY. *All re-
> treat in violent movement. 6 steps forward as
> Narrator.*]

6: During the night the troops surrounded the
    village
There was the Chief of Post with all his people
to find the men and fetch them from their huts
Just as they were when shaken out of sleep
naked and exposed
they had to line themselves up in a row
The Chief of Post next called the names on the
    list
and each one had to answer by his name
Then the men were loaded on the bed of a truck

> [*1, 2, 3, 4 to* THE BOGEY. *In* CHORUS.]

CHORUS: We women of Cabinda
are standing before the prison
we carry clothing for our husbands
You sirs Policemen
we want to see our husbands
to bring their clothing

> [*7 behind* THE BOGEY.]

7: They won't need it any longer

CHORUS: An airplane flew with what was
left of our husbands in sacks
far out over the sea
After days the tide then washed

back what was left onto the beach
Arms legs the torsos
     [*5 puts on a tropical helmet.*]
5: In Angola everything is calm
     [*7 steps forward. He also wears a tropical hel-
met.*]
7: In Angola nothing
has changed whatsoever
     [*5 goes to right next to 7. 6 goes left. In the
middle 1, 2, 3, 4 as* CHORUS.]
5: An investment of capital
in Angola is a good idea
The labor force there is a simple
tool not more and not less
The dividends on investment
run to 30 percent a year
7: Diamonds
5: For the Anglo-American Diamond Company
For the Oppenheimer Group
For Morgan
For De Beers
For Guggenheim
For Ryan and the Forminiere
For the Union Miniere du Haut-Katanga
For the Guaranty Trust Bank
7: Diamonds
6: For the monopoly concessions
Tax free
No export duty
CHORUS: Diamonds
6: A million carats a year
CHORUS: [*with 6 as soloist*] Diamonds
24,000 men in the diggings
24,000 men at forced labor in the diggings
24,000 men scratch for your diamonds
in the pits of Luanda and Lunda
for an annual pay

          of 200 dollars

3 AND 4: [*alternately*] Swamp frog snaps at the swarming
            gnats
          Gimme a centavo
          The golden plover digs worms out of the bark
          100 centavos in an escudo
          Bees suck honey out of the mango blossoms
          With one escudo I don't have enough

       7: Oil

       5: For the Lobito Fuel Oil Company
          For Petrofina
          For Royal Dutch Shell
          For the Burnay Bank
          For the First National City Bank

CHORUS: Oil

       6: Two million barrels each year

       1: Small and round our own huts
          of clay and straw
          Round the silvery houses of oil
          shining in the sun
          Trampled are our villages
          here the oil lives now
          Flows through the pipelines
          where once was the path
          With bare hands
          we put up our huts
          Gigantic machines came in
          to build the houses of oil
          High round shining houses
          the children stand about and stare

       7: Iron ore

       5: For the Companhia Mineira do Lobito
          For the Krupp Enterprise
          For Bethlehem Steel
          For Westminster Bank

CHORUS: Iron ore

       6: Three million tons each year

CHORUS: [*with 6 as soloist*] Iron ore copper asphalt
      manganese
      50,000 men in the pits
      50,000 men at forced labor in the pits
      50,000 men for you at the pits
      of Cuima Cassanga Saia Quitoba
      Quissaquele Tumbi Gungungo

2: In the dark
      in a heavy line
      workers from the barracks
      beside them on the tracks
      empty iron-ore cars
      In the dark
      back from the shafts
      the line of workers
      Next to them on the tracks
      the fully loaded iron-ore cars

CHORUS: See the rolling ore cars
      the puffing locomotives
      spraying sparks and whistling
      on the way through the forests
      down to the harbors

7: Coffee

5: For the Companhia Agricola de Angola
      For the Companhia Agricola do Cazengo
      For the Companhia Angolana de Agricultura
      For the Bank Rallet et Cie

CHORUS: Coffee

6: 200,000 tons a year

CHORUS: [*with 6 as soloist*] Coffee sisal sugar tobacco
      500,000 women and children on the plantations
      500,000 women and children at forced labor on
          the plantations
      500,000 women and children bringing in your
          harvest
      on the plantations of Benguela Cabinda Bie
      Cuanza Uige Zaire Moxico Huila

6: For 150 dollars a year
4: See the porters on the dock
working in long rows
See the cranes
They swing their loads
down into the ships
See the gentlemen on the dock
their faces otherwise so pale
are red
Eagerly they cross off
the items on their lists
See the smoke
pour from the stacks
Hear the turbines
Hear the sirens
The birds flee

SCENE VII

[*6 steps forward.*]
6: Farmers forced-laborers prisoners
Your gold
hangs on the neck of Europe
The masks of your ancestors
decorate Europe's State rooms
The produce of your earth
is digested
in Europe's belly
Deceived exploited hungering
By your labor
you have laid the foundation
of Europe's wealth
With your iron
Europe now arms itself
against you
1: At this hour

everywhere
about this our land
occupied by the enemy
we are getting together
to make ready
for our liberation

3: At this hour
everywhere
in a camp site of the deep forest
in a village hut
in a shack of the suburb
in a warehouse at the harbor
in the basement of a factory
we make the plan
of the uprising
[*1, 2, 3, 4 as* Chorus.]

Chorus: Excluded from all the
legal possibilities of resistance
threatened at every instance
the enemy is forcing us
to grasp upon the identical means
that he applies against us
[*5 and 7 move to near the* Chorus. *6 too joins
the* Chorus.]

5: What we demand is simple
and easily understood

All: That the land should belong
to those who work it
That the houses should be lived in
by those who build the houses
That the products should be used
by those who produce products
That the schools should be open
to everyone
[*There is a sudden change in the attitude of
the group. They will represent Colonizers. Pan-
tomime of a cocktail party. 7 steps to the side.*

Conversation in the group.]
What do you suppose they can accomplish
Their tribes are all
mixed up with feuding
They have no education
They haven't even a common language
If their leaders want to
reach an agreement
they have to do it
with our language
Truly
our policy was wise
        [*7, with microphone, as Announcer.*]
7: 1,000 men and women
from the localities of Bengo and Icolo
are on the way to Catete
to the District Office
They will seek to demand
the liberty of their leaders
200 soldiers are waiting for them
Without a warning there were shots
The dead and the wounded
sprawl in the streets
        [*Drumbeats imitate the bursts of a machine
        gun. The group scatters and sinks to the
        ground. A creeping and running in slow mo-
        tion. A picture of collapse and terror. Isolated
        cries from 3.*]
7: The prison and the police station
of Luanda
are assaulted by a popular crowd
Fighting rages
in the native quarter of Luanda
Sao Paulo
Tanks and parachutists
stand ready
The provinces of Cuanza and Luanda

are in upheaval
The dockworkers of Lobito and Mossamedes
are out on strike
The workers in the Cuima pits
are presenting demands
The oil lines to Luanda
as well as bridges and railroads
between Luanda and Malanje
have been blown up
[*7 puts aside the microphone. Steps forward.*]
7: This is the 15th of March 1961
Make a note of the date
The struggle for our independence
has begun

1, 2, 3,
4, 7: [*as the* CHORUS, *with 6 as soloist*]
In the cities
His power fails
In the villages
His power fails
In the fields
His power fails
On the coasts
His power fails
Drive him
Drive him back
where he came from
Drive him
Drive him back
into the sea
[*6 from the visage of* THE BOGEY. *With a ter-
rific strain of energy.*]
BOGEY: My dear officers
I have called you gentlemen together
for an assignment
which requires that
you strike the word compassion

from your memory
We do not fight against men
we fight against
untamed beasts
    [3 *triumphant.*]
3: They drive out the plantation owners
They plunder the houses and companies
They murder and they rape
    [1, 2, 4, 6 *as* CHORUS.]
CHORUS: Eat until you burst
Eat and drink
Drink the wine
Drain the barrels
Eat the roast golden hen
the roasted turkey
Pineapples and melons
Eat
till you fall from the table
BOGEY: Thanks to our aerial bridge with the mother
    country
we now have 25,000
men under arms
We are forming a white front
against anarchy
and terror
    [3 *triumphant.*]
3: They've taken the owner of a sawmill
and his family
and tied them to the boards
and run them lengthwise
through the buzz saw
7: I will laugh the bark off the trees
I will swim straight up the waterfall
I will dance the rocks to pieces
I will sing the lion dead
I will blow out the moon
BOGEY: Root them out

    wherever you find them
    Knock their damn heads off
    Stab the heads
    up on stakes
2: And it was no joke for the Western observers in
        the know
    for in Angola didn't Portugal defend their
        possession also
    And they knew that Portugal should not come
        knocking in vain
    if it ever should raise a request for credits again
        [1, 3, 4, 6 as CHORUS.]
CHORUS
  AND 2: For they all felt themselves bound by contract
        as true partners in the Atlantic Pact
    2: And they delivered by millions their dollars
        deutschmarks and pounds
    Not only that their military help also made the
        rounds
    Portugal had not long to look about and wonder
    before came the warships good trucks and aerial
        thunder
CHORUS
  AND 2: For they all felt themselves bound by contract
        as true partners in the Atlantic Pact
    7: Dig the bullet out of my guts
    Set my head back on
    Sew my arm to me
    Bind on my leg
    so that I
    can be with you again
    2: There never before had been shipments of
        foodstuffs or tractors
    but now at the Azores base of the American
        benefactors
    There landed such gifts as the African peoples
        never desired

even if by the donators and their allies greatly
required

CHORUS

AND 2: For they all felt themselves bound by contract
as true partners in the Atlantic Pact

2: Then next one saw the brave pilots of Portugal
hurry to drop the gifts on the population over-all
And the world in the West looked on with
strong satisfaction
and as those fires burned expressed no adverse
reaction

CHORUS

AND 2: For they all felt themselves bound by contract
as true partners in the Atlantic Pact
[*4 springs forward. Alternates with* 1, 2, 3, 6, 7
as the CHORUS.]

4 AND

CHORUS: The fire falls from the sky
The fire eats up the forest
The fire falls from the sky
The fire eats up the village
The fire falls from the sky
The fire eats up our women
The fire falls from the sky
The fire eats up our children

2: For the Western observers it was like igniting a
scrap pile
with the elephant grass and the bush ablaze and
all this while
the number of black corpses mounted but our
onlookers were not troubled
be the casualties 30,000 or that figure doubled

CHORUS

AND 2: For they all felt themselves bound by contract
as true partners in the Atlantic Pact

2: And it didn't matter how many prisoners were
locked up out of sight

surely soon they would perish from hunger and
  thirst all right
Only those 500 dead Lusitanian soldiers their
  peers
gave the West a pause sufficient to unleash their
  tears
        [1, 3, 4, 6, 7 *represent a grotesque procession.*
        6 with Bishop's hat. They pantomime the lay-
        ing of a wreath. For the wreath, a bicycle
        wheel.]
CHORUS
  AND 2: For they all felt themselves bound by contract
      as true partners in the Atlantic Pact
        [THE BOGEY *during the wreath-laying cere-*
        mony. With sepulchral voice.]
BOGEY: We have now mustered
      50,000 men in arms
      We are masters of the situation
      The mob that was led to uprising
      through blindness and agitation
      has been routed and dispersed
      Not more than a few isolated bands remain
        active
      and they have fled off to the forests
      Aside from these no tokens of
      struggle may be noted
        [6 *preaching. The others at prayer.*]
    6: We shall carry on with the task
      of Civilizing and Christianizing
    7: [*praying*]
      This region's peoples shall be led
      from the paths of their ignorance
        [THE BOGEY's *sepulchral voice heightened by*
        an echo effect.]
BOGEY: The crisis was difficult yes
      but we have known how to survive it
      with God's own help

and our own firm resolve
And if the question be asked
Have we achieved anything
with the money of the plain man
with our soldiers' blood
with the tears of mothers
then I shall answer
Yes
Not only our own
legitimate property
but additionally the welfare of the world
we have been defending
in Angola
    [*Big yawn.*]
6: O you spawn of a noble nation
Splendidly you have reaped honor
while bearing the Gospel of God
implacably across the oceans
even to the peoples
of the most distant continents

SCENE VIII

[*7 represents a foreign high-ranking Minister of Justice on a visit to Lusitania's African provinces. 1, 2,
3, 4 in a circle about him. His words are gratefully
received.*]
7: I will speak only
of what I have seen with my own eyes
I saw only progress
in Lusitania's African provinces
Angola and Mozambique
I saw only islands of peace
For centuries the equality
of rights between the races
has prevailed here

Without exercising the least force
the mother country has opened
to every Black
the opportunity
of all forms of education
The man without means
can study at the State's expense
All offices are
open to everybody
Even the Mayor
can be a Black
Such is the case
in Nampula
a rising industrial city
of Mozambique
      [1, 2, 3, 4 *form the* CHORUS.]
CHORUS: There would have been great laughter from the
     6 million of Mozambique
had not even one of them climbed to be Mayor
     that mighty peak
Pedro Baessa chooses the latest style of shoes and
     clothing
and asks for compliance with whatever the
     government's got going
smokes good cigars with white citizens and drinks
     their ales
and turns up at solemn occasions in his medals
     and tails
The whole world may judge from this single
     sample
why Portugal rates so highly as a colonial
     example
7: Of colonial force
I could not detect
the least suggestion
In any case the phrase
Foreign Rule

is simply not applicable
to territories that have stood
under Portugal's guidance
for half a thousand years now
Some fanatic groups do still
carry on with their troublemaking
Apart from that the white
visitor meets only friendly
and grateful faces
Not Portugal
threatens the world's peace
in Africa
and let me make this clear
and emphatic
The danger today
comes only and alone
from without

> [*7 departs. 1, 2, 3, 4 at once redispose them-*
> *selves. They pantomime women working in the*
> *fields.*]

3: Where are the men of Mozambique
Why are there no men to be found
in the villages and in the fields
of Mozambique

> [*1, 2, 4 as* CHORUS.]

CHORUS: Our men have gone far away
across the borders
For longer than a year
we have not been able to see our men
For longer than a year
we have not heard
anything from our men
Our men have not given us any clothing
Our men have not
even given us
a black square of cloth

3: Why aren't they here

the men of Mozambique

CHORUS: The men were taken off
and do not know where they will go
Only the masters of the pits
in South Africa Rhodesia and Katanga
know where they will go
And our authorities know
where they will go
and the authorities get a head-price
6 dollars for every man
and our authorities receive a half
of each man's wages
and only when our men return
do they get this pay
after the tax is taken
The authorities have an 18-month contract
system
which tightly binds the men
of Mozambique to the pits
of South Africa Rhodesia and Katanga
And many of our men never come back
dead of their injuries
weakness and sickness
in those pits
of South Africa Rhodesia and Katanga
Their wages are collected
by our authorities
300,000 men of Mozambique
dig gold coal and iron
for the pit masters
of South Africa Rhodesia and Katanga

SCENE IX

[*5 appears in* THE BOGEY. *Now wearing the shoulder decorations of the General. Feeble. But makes
the best of it.*]

BOGEY: Now we have 55,000
men in arms in Angola
We have in Mozambique
40,000 men
Guinea
20,000 men
We have held
and we shall continue to hold

> [*5 closes the hatch. 6 enters wearing tail coat
> and the mask of a fox. Represents a foreign
> Bank Director in Lusitania on official business.
> Accompanied by 7. Wears dark glasses. The
> right arm stiffly raised. A black glove on the
> hand. Under the other arm a briefcase. 1 sings
> into a microphone cabaret style.*]

1: Let us now see how a mighty controller of great
banks
closes out his deals owing to others mighty
thanks
What he pays out always is less than comes in
but from the start it was ever this way for him
For he's found nothing with so much allure
as the money he's looted from the poor

> [*6 and 7 go up to* THE BOGEY. *In the open visor
> 5 again appears. Now he wears the mask of a
> vulture. A grotesque greeting.*]

1: Where the conquerors ruled with a competent
will
there he'd come in with his more than special
skill

With his transactions he helped in the conquest
regardless of the results everything for him always
    turned out best
      [2, 3, 4 join in on the refrain]
For he's found nothing with so much allure
as the money he's looted from the poor
      [6 scampers up to The Bogey.]
6: It is for me a great and keen pleasure
  to reaffirm our fine business relations
  with an additional loan
  of 170 million deutschmarks
  You also can regard this decision
  as a return favor
  for the humane sympathy
  and unusual sense of justice you displayed
  after the last war
  when the uncollected payments due us
  were on Your Majesty's own orders
  not confiscated
Bogey: Most estimable friend
  We long have been filled
  with admiration
  for your nation's
  great deeds and achievements
  and our common bond with you
  offers the most certain guarantee
  of a successful outcome to our struggle
  against this world's
  destructive forces
      [Big yawn. 5 comes from behind The Bogey
      yawning. Starts to dance with 6. 5 stiff and un-
      steady. Caws occasionally.]
1: And in case the conquerers were thrown down
    and blasted were the nations
  our manipulator had everything arranged to
    guard his own share of rations

Nor was he one who feared to find his path
   barricaded
for in his Cause other mighty figures stood
   initiated
     [*2, 3, 4 join in the refrain*]
For he's found nothing with so much allure
as the money he's looted from the poor
1: They only had to mention this man's our very
   own
   in order to put him back on his feet if he
   needed a loan
   That's why he turns up wherever there's a profit
   for the making
   He will always be there prepared with an artful
    economic undertaking
     [*2, 3, 4 join in the refrain*]
   For he's found nothing with so much allure
   as the money he's looted from the poor
     [*As they pantomime the pickpocketing of each*
     other, 5 caws, to the yips and throaty growls
     of 6.]
5: As a token of the
   friendly links between our States
   we are placing at your disposal
   airfields at Beja to the extent of 2,000 acres
   also education facilities depots
   camps and hospitals for your troops
   What is more the port of Casteloes
   shall be for the use of your fleet
   and the industries of Alverca
   shall make material
   for your army exclusively
   This offers much advantage
   since even in peacetime
   all of this can be kept
   ready for the use
1: Thus do all things stand at his disposition

just as they should in our Banker's best tradition
While the Western world stands united at his
   back
for it understands what he intends by this tack
      [2, 3, 4 *in refrain*]
For he's found nothing with so much allure
as the money he's looted from the poor
      [5, 6, 7 *dance off, 6 supporting 5, who is near*
      collapse.]

1: In good time once again he's on hand
to help all new powers that be to stand
And to fit their purposes with a machinery
that allows them to seize on each opportunity
      [2, 3, 4 *in refrain*]
For he's found nothing with so much allure
as the money he's looted from the poor

SCENE X

[5 *and* 7 *return without the masks. All disposed in*
a wide rank. All lie down or squat, except 5. 5 *in*
the center, standing stiff and straight. The quiet
continues for a time.]

5: Today
through every prison of the land the
unrest has spread
From Aljube to Tarrafal
the report got around
the Deceiver was going to die
From cell to cell
we tapped out
this gospel news
      [4 *is prone, speaks with great difficulty.*]

4: For Portugal everything is getting steadily
better

The economic development
goes forward on the basis
of a healthy currency
The circulation of the escudo
is 131 percent guaranteed
with gold and foreign exchange
     [3 *speaks tonelessly.*]
3: In Fort Peniche
the water runs down off the walls
After a rainfall
the water stands
above our ankles
In Fort Peniche
there are no windows
We lie upon the boards
beneath a moldy blanket
In the nights we hear the cries
of the tortured
4: Never
has the foreign trade with our land
reached such a point
as in this year
The real-estate agencies are swamped
with the inquiries of the interested
from all corners
of the Free World
1: [*softly, anguished*]
They call this
standing statue
You stand an entire day
an entire night
You can't go to sleep
if you do they throw in a pail of water
and another entire day
and another entire night
Your legs swell up
Your heart beats wildly

You can't fall down
if you do they throw in a pail of water
You can't stand any longer
but you must another entire day
and another entire night
    [*Pause.*]
1: On the fourth day
the hallucinations begin
I hear the voices
of the thousands
in Fort Peniche
I no longer feel my legs
I don't sleep
I'm not awake
I hear the voices
of the hundred thousands
in the prisons
I stand
not moving
    [*7 gets up with a great effort.*]
7: A growing role is played by foreign capital
in our exports-oriented private enterprise
due to a favorable costs-to-profits ratio
And as they say in Lisbon
Would leading European
and American industries
increase their investments in
our African provinces
if they were not persuaded
of our future
in these territories
    [*6 slowly lifts the creaking lid from the face of*
    The Bogey. *6 squeezes into his speech the last*
    ounce of strength before a final silence. As The
    Bogey *speaks the other players rise slowly.*
    Their demeanor in every way is expressive of
    rage and rebellion.]

BOGEY: And if we hold this territory
        for yet another decade
        then we shall finally
        have won the struggle
        for within 10
        to 15 years
        the so-called
        sovereign Africa
        shall disappear in chaos
        for it is not capable
        of governing itself
            [*5 shouts.*]
5: Well look at this old man
    just look at this cold man
    who'd like to hold his grip here and
    thinks he can
        [*7 likewise.*]
7: Look how his face is thin
    why look at his gray skin
    he dreams that we shall always be
    serving him
        [*The attitude of all becomes increasingly menacing. They turn upon* THE BOGEY. *6 has vanished behind* THE BOGEY. *The visor stands wide open.*]
4: Look at this man of straw
    look through that empty maw
    he has nothing left except
    a shadow of his law
        [*All accompany the song with outcries, calls and leaps. They approach* THE BOGEY.]
2: Look at this man spurned
    give him what he's earned
    what in these 5 centuries
    we forcibly learned
5: Strike hard this pallid man
    strike down this squalid man

that to be here among us again
he never can

> [*All fall upon* THE BOGEY. *Tear the honorary
> ribbon, sword and billy-club from him. Form
> into a chain and pull at the great figure. Be-
> hind, 6 releases the mechanism that holds it
> upright. The great figure falls over. With a
> mighty crash it topples to the ground. The ped-
> estal proppings are empty. Some straw dangles.
> The sack flutters. All motionless and quiet for
> a moment. Then 1 steps forward. All draw
> themselves up.*]

1: Even though it's now said that he's dead
he who in our very land kept us long in dread
do not be deceived his hand is still everywhere
events are repeating themselves let's not be
  unaware

5: [*softly*]
We the prisoners damn the night
which made our land helpless beneath the blight

1: Now we have Generals who are the profiteering
  wheelers-and-dealers
who have their police and soldiers and treasury-
  stealers
While the Western partners have slipped back
  by stealth
to take their share in the defense of a stolen
  wealth

7: [*softly*]
We the prisoners curse each single day
that our land cannot yet act to drive them away

> [*6 enters from left with the little curtain. 1
> helps him to hold it. From behind, 2 steps
> through the curtain, her face drawn into a false
> smile. Sings to an insinuating melody.*]

2: So patiently working you see our agricultural
  people

frivolous riches have no lure for them
Contented they dwell in their villages so clean
Humility binds them to the great landowners
those whose manor houses lend dignity to the
    landscape
      [*2 steps to the right toward the others. Speaks
      harshly now.*]

2: But don't you get lost and wander down those
    stony paths
that lead to the shanties where we have to live
Just keep your eye on the splendid boulevards
else you start in to hear mid the garbage and
    crowds
another voice one of rage and revolt
      [*3 steps through the curtain from behind. Pulls
      her face into a false smile. Sings the insinuating
      melody.*]

3: Enriched by this glimpse into a people's soul
enlivened by a stroll through the blooming
    garden
and the hours on a beach in the refreshing
    breezes
you come into Lusitania's hospitable cities
which offer you their treasures of the most
    splendid art
      [*3 remains standing in front of the curtain. 5
      speaks harshly.*]

5: But don't you walk inside those pompous edifices
where we stand before judges who're bought and
    sold
and where we're condemned hour after hour
workers and students clerical types too
who want a different Lusitania than this

CHORUS
OF ALL: And there shall be more
    you will see them
    Many already in the cities

and in the forests and mountains
laying in their weapons and planning with care
the Liberation
which is near

Discourse
on the Progress
of the Prolonged War of Liberation
in Viet Nam
and the Events Leading Up to It
as Illustration of the Necessity
for Armed Resistance Against Oppression
and on the Attempts
of the United States of America
to Destroy the Foundations
of Revolution

Each actor in this play represents a number of figures whose statements and behaviour as a whole typify a particular historical development. The figures represented give expression to individual experience as well as to general aspects. Sometimes they are persons identifiable in history, sometimes anonymous representatives of various groups known to have existed. The individual spokesmen for these groups convey, both personally and collectively, actual problems and conflicts. Those identified with a name are not characters in the usual sense: they are named simply as representatives of significant tendencies and interests. Choruses are introduced when attention is to be drawn in more detail to particular reactions. The aim is to present figures bound up in historical processes, even when it is a matter of historical developments of which the participants were themselves not aware. An attempt is made to present a succession of social stages, with all their essential features and discrepancies, in such a way that they throw light on the conflict existing today.

Even though the figures in this play show nothing of their personal characteristics and private lives, they must not be interpreted in an abstract way. The actors should strive to present them in real terms as active human beings who have altered the course of history. Transition from one role to another is not effected by masks and costumes: it is simply hinted at by the use of single attributes, i.e., a helmet, a shield, a weapon, a shawl, a piece of jewellery or of uniform. The principal means of indicating a change of role are through a change of position, new groupings or different ways of speaking and moving. To identify specific historical power groupings, flags are used here and there, in the form of shields. Weapons and other emblems are also employed. All figures from the early and late phases of the history of Viet

Nam and feudal China wear simple black costumes of a uniform cut. Representatives of the colonial powers, as well as of their vassals in Viet Nam, wear the same white costume. Accessories such as shoulder straps, decorations, military caps, etc., are also white. In the few cases where colour is used, this should be very strong and glaring.

The stage area is white, and as much of the stage as possible should be used. A square shape would be the most advantageous. Stretching right across the back of the stage there is a narrow raised area; on both sides long white platforms. These are in several parts and can be easily taken apart and used for the table required in Part Two of the play. There is full, bright lighting throughout.

The figures move within the framework of the points of the compass, as indicated: N, NE, E, SE, S, SW, W, NW. In Part One the geographical points of the stage correspond to a large extent with the actual geographical relationships: China can be assumed to be in the north, Funan and Champa in the south, and Viet Nam in the centre. Since there is neither scenery nor the usual sort of stage furniture, the actors have nothing to rely on but their own movements, positionings, relationships to one another, groupings and regroupings. Absolute precision is essential in following prescribed paths, in taking up and leaving positions, in observing their relationships with one another, in the formation of groups and in maintaining the varying tempi of each scene. Forms of expression must be chosen that reduce the attitudes of individuals or groups to something general and typical of all. This precision of movement is necessary because the aim is to convey an exact picture of power relationships between groups, parties and states, in geographical as well as other aspects.

The stage directions as here printed are designed to make perfectly clear the necessity of presenting the play with the utmost simplicity. By dispensing with costume and restricting outward appearances to the barest decorative details, actors are reminded that they must make words, gestures and groupings the main means of communication. In speaking the text, the actors must pay particular attention to the line divisions.

The incidental music, where indicated, should not strive to be illustrative, and on no account should it sound exotic. Here too the utmost simplicity is called for—rhythmic rather than melodic.

The play requires 15 actors, each marked in the text with the figures 1 to 15. Two of them—5 and 6—are female. Two assistants, A and B, bring required articles on and off stage. If required, two further assistants may be employed.

A slide projector and a loudspeaker are required in Part Two.

The play was first performed on March 20, 1968, at the Städtische Bühnen, Frankfurt am Main.

Director: Harry Buckwitz. Settings and costumes: Gunilla Palmstierna-Weiss. Choreographic associate: Jean Soubeyran. Music: Peter Schat.

Actors: Rudolf Plent, Jodoc Seidel, Peter Fitz, Fritz Nydegger, Ursula Mörger, Kirsten Dene, Mogens von Gadow, Hansjoachim Krietsch, Gerhard Retschy, Hans Otto Ball, Werner Eichhorn, Wolfgang Hinze, Joachim Böse, Frank Rehfeldt, Jurgen Hilken. Assistants: Michael Habeck, Winfried Küppers, Peter Brombacher, Claus Fuchs. Drummers: Karl Görner, Reinhard Schneider.

PART ONE

PHASE I

[*14, 15 as natives of Funan in central area* W. *7, 8 as Chinese travellers come slowly from NE to central area. 7, 8, 14, 15 all dressed in black. 7, 8 are accompanied by assistants A and B, who hold large oars, which they move slowly.*]

7: We come from the port of Hangchou
Favourable winds led us across the seas
We have heard of the wealth of the land
   by the Mekong
     [*7, 8 advance farther towards SW and turn to 14, 15.*]

8: Before us the kingdom of Funan
Many ships have come to meet us
Many ships give us escort

7: Behind earthworks and towers a large city
The moats filled with crocodiles
The houses on stilts
Canals flow through the city

8: The people unclothed
dark of skin
     [*7, 8 step ashore. A and B remain in the background, leaning on their oars.*]

7: A palace with carved pillars
Nobles in rose-coloured silk
girdles and earrings of gold

8: We have heard
you have spices and aromatic woods
We have heard

of your ivory and your pearls
7: Your copper and your gold
14: What do you bring for us
8: We bring your king lacquered caskets
fans and sunshades
14: The king will not receive you
He has turned his back on earthly things
7: We have heard of the fame of your king
who is called King of the Mountains
8: A temple with gilded towers
7: The walls set with jewels
[*Chinese travellers 7, 8 with expressions
of admiration for the buildings described.*]
14: The tomb of the former king
The godly one has left the lower world
and entered the state of blessedness
Gone is the time when as a mortal man
he watched over the observance of eternal
laws
8: They must be mighty kings
to have tombs as high as mountains
14: For the living kings slaves erect
tombs reaching up to heaven
so they may easily come to Nirvana
7: They must be mighty gods
to be honoured with such temples
15: The kings interpret the wishes of the gods
At the king's command
we cut canals and raise up dams
Thus we turn swamps and brackish waters
into fertile land
The kings tell us how to build ships
with which we sail the seas
14: Nothing happens except
as the mighty gods will it
15: The laws of our fathers are unalterable
[*The Chinese travellers 7, 8 turn in direc-*

> *tion NW. A soft processional music begins.*]

7: We hear them give thanks as they bring in
   the harvest
   We hear their prayers as they sail out to
   fish
   We see them filling the king's granaries
   > [*1, 2, 3, 4, 5 pass slowly along the raised
   > level at the back from NW to NE. 1, 2,
   > 3, 4, 5 dressed in black. They depict a pro-
   > cession, carrying simple emblems of pomp
   > and power. 14, 15 bow low.*]

8: In Funan the fishermen and peasants fall
   silent
   They bow down before the procession
   as it comes through the gates
   The king is moving to another palace
   He is hidden
   in the golden litter on the elephant's back
   Drums and flags go with him
   > [*The procession goes off NE. The music
   > ends.*]

7: In the palaces and temples the treasures
   pile up

8: In the villages there is hunger
   The people are in the mountains
   dragging down stones for the buildings
   Their fields will go to rot
   > [*7, 8 start the return journey. Assistants
   > A and B follow them, moving their oars
   > as before. 7, 8 and assistants A and B in
   > direction NE. 14, 15 slowly in direction
   > SW. 9, 10, 11, 12, 13 come from direction
   > NW as peasant soldiers from China. 9,
   > 10, 11, 12, 13 dressed in black. 9, 10 wear
   > hooded helmets; 11 carries a spear.*]

7: The jungle will grow over the land of
Funan
The jungle will destroy all the buildings
[*The soldiers 9, 10, 11, 12, 13 form an ex-
tended line in N. The natives of Funan
14, 15 go off SW. 7, 8 have reached the
end of their journey. 7, 8, and assistants
A and B go off NE.*]

9: Everywhere
between the Yellow River and the Yangtze
fighting has broken out
[*Group 9, 10, 11, 12, 13 as peasant soldiers march forward to centre from N.
Mimed representation of armed raids.*]

11, 12, 13: No land for us in China
So we have joined the army
Here we can find ourselves land

10: We fight our way across the river Hoan Ho

9: What do we find in the land of the Wei

10: No more land than there is at home

13: But the little there is
we take for ourselves

11: All who will not give up their land
are slaughtered

12: The soil parched

9: The harvest ruined

10: Famine in the villages
Let us move on to Chou
[*The soldiers wheel round violently in di-
rection NE.*]

11: There the fields are full of rice
[*The soldiers push forward towards NE.
Towards them from NE come 14, 15 as
Chinese peasants. 14, 15 dressed in black.*]

14: They are setting our villages on fire

15: They are robbing our granaries

[*The soldiers move off violently in direction NW.*]

14, 15: Two hundred thousand people
have been beheaded in Chou
[*14, 15 go off in direction N. From NE 1, 2, 3, 4, 5, 6 come in as people from the Viet in Van Lang. They form a close group.*]

1, 2, 3: We peasants and hunters
of the people of Viet
live in the southern regions of the Yangtze

5: Our country is called Van Lang

6: Our king is wedded
to the daughter of the Great Sea-dragon

4: One hundred sons
have been born to our king
from the sea

1: Our land has a hundred principalities.
[*Group 9, 10, 11, 12, 13 as peasant soldiers from the NW advance threateningly towards the Viet group. 14, 15 as Chinese warriors join the peasant soldiers. 14 indicates the Viet group.*]

14: The land of the Viet is fertile
the rivers stocked with fish
[*Aggressive movement from the group of Chinese soldiers. The Viet group in defensive positions.*]

2: The Wu armies threaten our land
[*The group of soldiers moves violently into the Viet group, which scatters.*]

4, 5, 6: The Wu armies occupy our country

2: They take away our harvest

1: They rob us of our fish

4: They plunder our barns

3: They force us into their army

5: Our princes are no match for the enemy

4: The enemy has better weapons
      [*The Viet group comes together in a close
      formation. Behind them in N the soldiers
      form up in a half circle.*]
3: We will leave our land
   rather than submit to them
4: Our forefathers are buried here
6: The spirits of our ancestors will accompany
   us
4, 5: With our hundred princes we shall travel
   south
2, 3: We shall find a country with a large river
1: We shall find a rich and fertile country
      [*The Viet group moves from NE in di-
      rection SW to the central area. The move-
      ment of the Viet group can be accom-
      panied by rhythmic sound effects. At the
      same time the Chinese soldiers complete
      the circle around the former position of
      the Viet group and plant an emblem of
      Chinese sovereignty there.*]
5: The hundred sons of the king
   lead us towards the south
3, 4: Fifty sons of the king
   lead us to the mountains
1, 2: Fifty sons of the king
   lead us to the valleys
      [*The Viet group comes to a standstill.*]
3: We have come to the valley of a great river
4: The water is full of fish
1: The woods are full of game
6: The soil is fertile
      [*The Viet group forms a semicircular
      chorus. Music begins.*]
CHORUS: Here the people of the Viet
   having left the central empire
   found the kingdom of Viet Lac

[*Music ends. The peasant soldiers 9, 10, 11, 12, 13 together with 14, 15 file off in NE. They leave the emblem of sovereignty behind. The Viet chorus quietly dissolves. From NW assistants A and B bring in various pieces of costume: a helmet for the king, a cloak for the princess, a few weapons. The group mimes the following fable.*]

6: The king is seeking a husband
for his daughter My Nuong
The god of the mountains and the god of
the sea
are paying court to her
Both equally handsome and strong
The king cannot decide between them

3: He who tomorrow brings me the richest
gifts
shall have my daughter

6: First comes the god of the mountains
bringing gifts of jade ivory and gold
such as the king has never seen before

3: To you I give the Princess My Nuong

1: The Princess My Nuong follows the god of
the mountains
Then comes the god of the sea
bringing gifts of mother-of-pearl
amber and coral
such as the king has never seen before

6: The Princess My Nuong is with the god of
the mountains

2: Then the god of the sea grows angry
He sends whirlwinds and storms across the
land
He throws floods across the land
every wave bearing soldiers

4: The soldiers storm the mountains

Then the god of the mountains grows angry
He sends thunder and lightning over the
     land
He throws cloudbursts over the land
every bush bearing soldiers
3: The battle rages long
The blood of the soldiers flows into the
     river
Since then the river is red from the soldiers'
     blood
6: Each year since then the god of the sea
     comes
and lashes the land with gales and floods
5: Each year since then the god of the
     mountains comes
and lashes the land with thunder and rain
     [*From NE 10, 11, 12 enter, dressed in
     black and wearing emblems of Chinese
     warlords. They move to the centre.*]
10: Shi Huang Ti has restored law and order
     everywhere
through the superior strength of his arms
11: Shi Huang Ti has proclaimed himself
     emperor
12: Shi Huang Ti has united all countries in a
     single empire
10: Shi Huang Ti has overthrown all the
     princes
11: Shi Huang Ti has appointed his loyal
     generals
governors over the provinces
12: Shi Huang Ti brings happiness
to all people on earth
10: Shi Huang Ti restores harmony
to both state and family
11: Shi Huang Ti makes learned men
officials of the state

12: Power and authority to the elders and
        betters
10: Subordinates must obey without question
11: The ideal concept is
10, 12: Humanity and justice
11: All to work
    in their appointed offices and ranks
    their professions and their serving places
    for the benefit of the state
10, 12: Personal property is inviolable
            [*10, 11, 12 go off in* NW. 7, 8, 9 *as Chi-*
            nese warriors come forward from NE *and*
            threaten the Viet group. 7 *with Chinese*
            breast armour, 8 *with helmet,* 9 *with*
            sword and bow. 8 *takes the emblem of*
            Chinese sovereignty and bears it before
            him.]
7: No land for us
    in the great central empire
8: So we must get land for ourselves
9: At the end of the road to the south
    there is free land
7: Fertile and cultivated soil
    There we can find land
        [*The Viet group turns towards the Chi-*
        nese warriors.]
4: We have built no ramparts
    We have not forged enough weapons
2: A traitor
    has snatched the Golden Tortoise's claw
    from the king's bow
5: The claw that made him invincible
        [*The group of Chinese warriors ap-*
        proaches the Viet group.]
9: The Golden Tortoise's claw
    is now mine
6: The stranger

has the Golden Tortoise's claw
[*The group of Chinese warriors forces it-*
self into the Viet group.]
5: The stranger has thrown the king
into the sea
4, 5, 6: A stranger
ascends the throne
[*9 receives the king's crown. 7, 8 are given*
the insignia of their new power.]
9: Now I belong to the people of Viet
I shall make this land strong
I shall protect this land
against the rulers of the north
I name this land
Nam Viet
which means
the land of the Viet in the south
8: As governor I shall ensure law and order
7: As prefect I shall ensure
that tributes and taxes
are regularly paid
9: You know the taxes are not
without purpose
The great discoveries of our ancient culture
will bring you benefit
[*7, 8, 9 form a separate group in* W. *They*
assume a raised position on the platform
and represent upper Nam Viet. The group
of Nam Viet people spread out far apart
in the centre.]
5: Overseers come to us in the villages
2: They watch over the gathering of the
harvest
1: They fix the taxes
6: We carry the rice
to the masters' granaries
3: We bring the masters our fish

4: For the masters we cut down trees

2: We forge weapons for them

7: We let you share
in the discoveries of our sciences

8: We instruct you in the arts
of poetry and painting

7, 8, 9: Your land has become our land
The northern border needs strong defense
The army must be reinforced
so that the enemy does not steal our harvest

6: Horsemen in armour are coming from the
north

8: Sound the gong in the soldiers' camp
[*5 goes to the group of leaders in W. Armour is put around her.*]

6: Princess Trung Trac
is summoning the army

4: The enemy has killed her husband
Now she is wearing his armour
With her sister Trung Nhi
she leads the army out to meet the enemy
[*From NE come 10, 11, 12 as heavily
armed Chinese warriors. Music. The group
of Nam Viet leaders 5, 7, 8, 9 moves in
close formation towards the group of Chinese warriors. The group of Nam Viet
people draws back towards S and watches
the battle. Mimed representation of the
battle. The fighters form a single in-
termingled group. Mechanical, repeated
movements. The fighting group moves in
direction W.*]

1: The enemy has mobile towers and slings

2: They are fighting in the valley of the river
Dai

1: Listen to the clashing weapons

4: Dark clouds in the sky

6: The clouds are covering up the sun

1: Our army is falling back

6: To the chalk cliffs

3: The cliffs are blocking the way

2: They are fighting at the cliffs

6: Fighting in the rain

4: The army is hemmed in at the cliffs

7: Trung Trac has thrown herself in the river

8: Trung Nhi has drowned herself in the river

2: Our army is defeated

1: They are cutting off
the princes' heads

> [*All weapons are raised in a simultaneous movement for the strike. 5, 7, 8, 9 fall to the ground. The Chinese warriors go to W to occupy the raised platform. They take the weapons and armour of the defeated with them. Music ends.*]

10: Such is the fate of all who dare
to set themselves up
against the mighty central empire

11: To avoid further unrest
let us divide the land into military districts

12: We shall strengthen the troops
in the citadels

> [*Weapons and decorative objects are hung on the wall in W by assistants A and B, to form an emblem of power. 7, 8, 9 are now together with 10, 11, 12 as the new feudal lords of Nam Viet. 5 goes to the group of Nam Viet people. Tableau: the new lords assume pompous attitudes. 2, 3, 5 come together at centre to form a chorus.*]

CHORUS: The land of our fathers
was invaded by strangers
Our fathers sought a new land

We live in the land that our fathers found
The land of our fathers is invaded by
    strangers
Our fathers see the junks of the strangers
sail out fully laden
The sacrificial dishes on the graves of our
    fathers
stand empty
Our fathers summon us
to free our land from the strangers
        [2, 3, 5 *move apart. The tableau in* W *dis-*
        solves.]

PHASE II

        [1, 2, 3, 4, 5, 6 *as group representing the peo-*
        ple of Nam Viet widely spaced in the centre.
        7, 8, 9, 10, 11, 12 *representing the feudal lords*
        of Nam Viet in W, *positioned in the form of*
        a projecting rampart.]
6: That's where the great lords live
4: The emperor's officials
2: We never see them
3: They send their delegates
    to us in the villages
        [7, 8 *as feudal lords from the group in* W
        to centre.]
7: Have you delivered all the baskets
    kept no rice back for yourselves
8: He has a basket of rice
    hidden in his hut
1: My children are hungry
7: Cut off his hands
        [7, 8 *return to group* W. 10, 11 *as feudal*
        lords mount the platform in W *and indi-*
        cate the group of people, who mime the

events now described.]

10: Look at those long rows
of carriers on the roads
The poles on their shoulders bend
under the weight of their loads

11: The harbours full of ships
loading goods for our court

10: For glory and wealth our residence is the
equal
of any court in the central empire

11: And our craftsmen are skilled
in making fine pictures
and choice jewellery

4: Behind those ornamented pillars
the mandarins live
They're said to be dressed in silk
and are wise beyond all knowledge
For every word they can paint a symbol

10: For the sons of the best
most loyal families the road to knowledge
stands open
The teaching of the masters shall enable
them
to support us in our heavy responsibilities

[*3, 4, 5 come together to form a chorus.*]

CHORUS: The paddy field is a pregnant woman
Do not frighten the sprouting rice
No axe blows no shouting in the fields
Do not call the dead or demons by name
The sprouting rice demands sustenance
Bring fruit and water to the fields
Do not frighten the rice when you gather it
Hold the sharp knife concealed at your back
Stoop low and cut unseen
Take care the sun does not glint
in the blade of the knife

[*3, 4, 5 move quietly out of chorus forma-*

tion. *8, 9, 12 as warriors of the feudal*
lords in Nam Viet, armed with helmets
and weapons, leave the group in W in di-
rection NE. The group of Nam Viet peo-
ple turns towards them. 7, 10, 11 remain
in W as feudal lords.]

6: Look
The soldiers are leaving the fortress
It is said
armies are coming from the north
    [*8, 9, 12 go off in NE.*]

2: They are fighting again at the Red River
    [*13, 14, 15 as Chinese warriors from NE*
    in direction SW to centre.]

4: See the army leaders
beneath their shades

1: The javelin throwers
with their helmets and shields

2: Thousands of foot soldiers
and horsemen
    [*Music starts.*]

13, 14, 15: From the mighty central empire
comes An Nam
An Nam
the pacifier of the south
An Nam
marches into Nam Viet
to restore the unity
of the empire
    [*Music ends. 13, 14, 15 force their way*
    into the group of feudal lords 7, 10, 11
    in the W. Simultaneous raising of weap-
    ons before the strike.]

5: There go our princes
in chains

6: We know what happens to the losers
    [*7, 10, 11 kneel down.*]

5: The executioners
cut off their heads
[7, 10, 11 *throw themselves to the ground.*]

13, 14, 15: Let this land be named
An Nam
after the pacifier of the south

1, 2, 3: An Nam
a shameful name
for our land

13: An Nam
province
under the rule
of the central empire
[7, 10, 11 *rise and join 13, 14, 15 as rulers*
of An Nam in a tight group in W. Their
positions are reminiscent of the rampart
formation. A spear and a sword are held
before them. 1, 2, 3, 4, 5, 6 as people of
An Nam move quickly to form a row at
centre.]

1: We have to build them castles
2: We have to make them better roads
3: We have to feed the foreign troops
4: They drive us to work with rods
[*Music starts.*]

1, 2, 3, 4: We sow the fields
We gather the rice
We sail the sea
and pull in the nets
We go to the mountains
and dig out the ore

5, 6: So it was in the year of the dragon
So it was in the year of the serpent
So it is now in the year of the rainbow

1, 2, 3, 4: We bring full baskets to the soldiers
We bring full baskets to the warlords
In the villages we starve

[*Music ends. The group of people dis-*
perses and takes up positions widely sepa-
rated from one another. 13, 14 from the
group of leaders in W walk slowly to cen-
tre. 13 wears a mandarin's cloak, 14 a hel-
met. Expansive, deliberate movements—
the warlords are visiting the people.]

13: In the fields
draught-oxen and reapers

14: The roads filled
with carts and bearers

13: In the factories timber
metals and busy tools

14: Ceaseless labour
for the common good

13: Lowly and fleeting
is the work of hands
Eternal
are the lofty thoughts of the masters

[*The two warlords have completed their*
tour and return to W. 7, 15 as warlords
move slowly to centre. 7 bejewelled, 15
armed. With the same superior gestures.]

7: From India we have brought in
silk and precious jewels
Life in our courts would be pleasanter still
if we could use all the produce of this land
for our trade

15: We have had many defeats
Our armies were too small
to break the power
of the central empire

7: With a hundred thousand men
we could do it
Behind every plough
behind every oar
there is a man

who could easily learn
to handle a lance or a sword
> *[The two leaders 7, 15 have completed*
> *their tour and return to W. 1, 2, 3, 4, 5, 6*
> *as peasants of An Nam form a close group*
> *in E. The warlords 13, 14, dressed as be-*
> *fore, move slowly towards E. Assistants A*
> *and B hold a canopy over them. The war-*
> *lords come to a stop before the group of*
> *people.]*

5: Now the warlords come more and more
often
to the villages in their litters
With their own eyes they look to see
that the taxes are paid in full

6: Look
The mandarin is leaning out from his litter

13: It is our declared wish
that equity shall prevail
in the fixing of the taxes
> *[The group of peasants draws back mis-*
> *trustfully. The leaders consult together.]*

14: We must make them understand
the validity of our aims

13: They cannot even speak our language

14: Then we must learn their language

13: We must teach them
that our fight for independence
from the central empire
is to their advantage too

14: In order to achieve our common goal
let us learn the peasants' language

13: Let us go into the villages
to tell the peasants
to what greatness this country can aspire
> *[The leaders approach the group of peas-*
> *ants again with ceremonious greetings.]*

5: The mandarins bow politely
   to the village elder

6: And praise the orderliness of the village

1: The mandarins speak the language of the
   villagers

4: The mandarins' visit
   is a great honour for us

2: The mandarins ask us
   to support the leaders in their struggle

3: A mandarin has never spoken to us
   like that before

13: You go hungry
    because the governors
    of the central empire
    demand their tributes

14: The tribute payments
    are a great burden on the land

13: Together with you
    we want to free the land
    from foreign domination

> [*The leaders 13, 14 go back to the* W.
> *From the group of peasants 1, 2 follow
> them and are given arms in the* W.]

3, 4, 5: The mandarins get better still
         in speaking the peasants' language

6: More and more peasants
   obey the mandarins' call

> [1, 2, 7, 10, 11, 13, 14, 15 *march off as an
> armed body in direction NE. They depict
> a battle on the raised level at the back as
> a tableau. 3, 4, 5, 6 as people of An Nam
> form a chorus. Music.*]

CHORUS: Under the command of the warlords
        the peasants fought
        against the armies of the central empire
        After many battles
        the warlords and the peasants

drove the enemy troops
back to the north
Our country is liberated
It shall be called for all time
Viet Nam

PHASE III

[*Quick dissolution of the battle tableau. Re-
grouping to represent a wall in N. 8, 9, 12
come from NE behind the wall. 9, with the
insignia of imperial power, is lifted up by 8,
12. The group of Viet Nam people, 3, 4, 5, 6,
far out at front, watch. Music.*]

5: There behind the walls
they are putting a new emperor
on the throne

[*The wall opens. Ceremonious procession
with symbols of pomp.*]

4, 6: The gates in the walls are opening

9: Before you appears
the mightiest and bravest
of all emperors

[*The procession moves towards the centre.*]

4: Band players and flag bearers
6: Servant girls with gold and silver
5: Elephants
3: Behind the screens
the emperor

3, 4, 5: He is raising a sword to the sky

8, 12: Down on your knees

[*The group of people at front bows down
respectfully. The procession disperses in
W. 9, 10, 11, 12, 13, 14, 15 remain in W
as the imperial court. 1, 2, 3, 4, 5, 6, 7, 8*]

*as Viet Nam peasants form a widely
spaced open group in E.*]

11: Heavy tasks await the emperor

13: Our northern borders must be held
against all
who try to invade the river valleys

9: Our southern borders must be extended
There lie the new territories we need

10: To carry out these tasks
landless peasants must be conscripted
into the army

> [*10, 13 are sent from the court into the
> villages. 10 with mandarin's robe, 13 with
> helmet. They approach the peasants.*]

1, 2: The mandarin is coming to our village
What does he want of us

13: Much time has passed since we drove the
foreigners out
Through your work you have helped
to raise our land to might and glory

10: The emperors in the goodness of their
hearts
have given you their land
to use in your own way
You reap your harvests three times in a year

13: And so your tributes to the emperor
must also be raised

3, 4: The harvests are rich
But you have taken
your share
Little remains
for us

13: We must be prepared
for great sacrifices
We must lay in stores

10: Arm ourselves for war
against the state of Champa

which threatens us in the south

13: All who do not pay their taxes
will lose their right to cultivate the land

7: We cannot afford higher taxes

10: You can send your sons to the army
instead

3: What is a soldier paid

10: Every soldier marching south
will be given a piece of land

13: The warrior's job is an honourable one
Promotion is open to all

> [*The leaders 10, 13 go back to W. From
> the peasant group 1, 2, 4 follow them.
> Music.*]

1, 2, 4: The private becomes a captain
The captain becomes a general
The general becomes a prince
who throws down the emperor
and takes the throne

> [*1, 2, 4 are given arms in W. Strong
> march rhythm. 1, 2, 4 as peasant sol-
> diers, 11 as warlord march off in direction
> SW. 12, 13, 14, 15 as professional soldiers
> march off from W in direction NE. The
> group of Viet Nam people 3, 5, 6, 7, 8
> form a circle in the centre. 9 as emperor,
> 10 as a Viet Nam leader remain on the
> platform W. The groups of soldiers plant
> their emblems in SW and NE. March
> rhythm ends.*]

1, 2, 4: We have overthrown enemy kings
We have killed their soldiers
We have burnt down their cities
and taken over their treasures
We have gained
a lot of new land

11: You must keep moving

   4: We were promised land of our own
  11: We must get to the valleys of the Mekong
   4: We want to cultivate the land
     to raise food for our families
   9: There can be no rest
     till all our enemies are beaten
   5: War is all we know
     We have not seen our sons for years
  10: We are not safe till we have taken
     the whole of Champa
   6: We are waiting for our sons
     to fetch us
     to the new land
     they have won
  12: Enemy horsemen are invading
     the valleys in the north
  13: The war junks of Kublai Khan
     in the Red River
9, 10: The northern border
     must be held
  14: The enemy has
     five hundred thousand men
  15: The enemy stands at the gates of Hanoi
  10: We have only two hundred thousand men
     in the north
   9: There are one hundred thousand
     in the south
  10: We need them to defend us
     from the Cham
   9: Then men and women everywhere
     must take up the fight
     against the enemy
     Leave your villages
     Leave your fields
     The harvest must not fall
     into enemy hands
       [The soldiers 12, 13, 14, 15 in NE fall

back. The group of Viet Nam people 3,
5, 6, 7, 8 hurry to help them. All together
they form a large group advancing in close
formation towards NE. As they advance,
9 as emperor of Viet Nam calls out.]

9: Protect the wealth
of our country
[*The advancing group in NE spreads out.*
Individual shouts from the group.]

6: We have liberated Hanoi

5: We have taken the enemy's guns

3: The enemy troops are massed together
Our groups are fast
and mobile

5, 6, 7: The enemy has never seen
soldiers like us before

8: Every citizen
a soldier

6: Children bringing food and messages

7: In every tree an archer

8: In every pass a trap

7: Surprise attacks by night

3, 7, 8: The mighty enemy army
torn to shreds

3: The enemy takes to its heels
[*Soldiers 1, 2, 4, 11 from SW to centre.*
To them the soldiers from NE and 9, 10
from W. Together they form a chorus.
Music.]

CHORUS: Historians shall record
in words that all can understand
how with one common effort
we drove back the mighty foe
[*Music ends. The chorus disperses. 11, 12,*
13, 14, 15 go off in NW and NE.]

PHASE IV

[1, 2, 3, 4, 5, 6, 7, 8 *as Viet Nam peasants*
form a wide group at centre. The individual
figures assume statuesque attitudes. 9, 10 as
Viet Nam leaders move freely between them.]

5: But many are missing from the villages
   Lie buried on the battlefields

4: I carry sand and stones in my basket
   to repair the dams

6: Here comes the landlord again
   demanding his taxes

10: The state needs funds
    to improve the administration
    and feed the army

3: We cannot pay taxes
   Our piece of land is not big enough

10: Then you must borrow money

8: We can't afford the interest

10: Then you must take on extra work
    to pay the interest

1: So we go on being serfs
   [*Music starts.*]

2, 4: We are being driven into the mines
   to dig out ore for the bosses

1, 7: We are being driven into the forests
   to cut wood for the bosses

6, 8: We are being driven down to the bed of
      the sea
      to bring up pearls for them
      [*Music ends.*]

3: Let us escape to the mountains
   [*With a single violent movement the*
   group of peasants breaks up and moves

*in flight in direction NW. 9, 10 back to
platform E.*]

2: We have come to the mountains
from all corners of the country
[*The group of rebel peasants moves in direction SE in a fan formation.*]

4: We march out in armed groups
to raid the landlords' granaries

1: We combine to form armies

3: We fight the landlords' mercenaries

4: They talk about one of our chiefs
in the northern mountains
who is spreading fear and terror
among the enemy
[*9, 10 in E lay down their symbols of office. 9 puts on the helmet of the warlord
Le Loi. 10 takes up weapons as his adjutant. Music.*]

3, 4, 5: He conjures soldiers out of every bush
Falls on the enemy from all directions
[*Music ends. Le Loi and his adjutant join
the ranks of the rebel peasants. The group
advances farther in direction SE.*]

8: The warlord Le Loi
drives out the princes and landlords

9: Chase them into the sea

10: Bring all the princes' treasures
to the warlord Le Loi
so that he can use them
to your advantage
[*All form a close group. In the middle at
front Le Loi and his adjutant.*]

1, 2, 4: The Emperor Le Loi in his justice
shares out the land
Every peasant gets his piece of land

5, 7: The Emperor Le Loi divides the land

                  among his generals and loyal followers
         3: He gives them the title of princes
         4: He divides the land
                  among his brothers and cousins
         9: Each receives land
                  according to his rank and his deserts
        10: The emperor commands
                  that a little plot of land
                  be given
                  to each peasant
  1, 2, 4: Le Loi is a strict
                  and just emperor
                  He has introduced
                  many new laws
                      [*Music starts.*]
  6, 7, 8: Three principles are to be observed
                  Honour the man of learning
                  Obey the military officer
                  Serve the mandarin
                      [*The music ends.*]
        10: The arts and sciences
                  blossom forth anew
                  Contests are held for poets
                  The schools are open to all
         3: Who can speak the Chinese language
        10: Everyone can participate
                  in examinations for public service
         3: If he is educated enough
         9: To further our great cultural projects
                  new taxes will be introduced
        10: Exempt from taxes from now on
                  Mandarins men of learning and priests
         9: Power and authority
                  to the elders and betters
        10: Absolute obedience
                  of the subordinate

9: All to work in their appointed offices and
       ranks
    for the welfare of the state
        [*The group dissolves. 9 as Le Loi and 10
        as his adjutant go to centre of the raised
        part N. 11 and assistants A and B come
        from NE. 7, 8, 11 and assistants A and B
        join 9, 10 to form royal court. Tableau of
        Chinese court manners. 1, 2, 3, 4, 5, 6 as
        Viet Nam peasants at front centre. Re-
        laxed movements.*]

1: A good harvest this year
    I saved two baskets of rice for myself

2: I still have my buffalo
    Next time the tax collector comes
    I shall hide it

6: On the day of rest
    we can fill the sacrificial bowls

3: My wife no longer has
    to bear her children out of doors
    I can build her a hut to lie in

4: For my daughter's wedding
    I've been given rice wine and a goat

5: My son is serving in Champa as a soldier
    I haven't heard from him for a long time

1, 2, 3,
4, 5, 6: May the spirits of our ancestors
    continue to smile on us
    May the spirits of the water and the fields
    continue to bring us good fortune
        [*The group of peasants forms a wide semi-
        circle. They sit down.*]

3: There were six animals
    Said the buffalo
    Without me no harvest
    I carry the rice to the barn

My hooves thresh the rice
Look at that useless dog
Does nothing but eat

2: Said the dog
I watch over you
No one dares come near
Even that horse fears me

1: Said the horse
I have freed the north
and pacified the south
My back bears warlords and princes
while that cock there
just scratches in the dungheap

5: Said the cock
It is I who wakes you
to the daily round
I am the herald of the morning sun
But look at that pig
lying snoring over there

6: Said the pig
· No one is as well nourished as I
Without me no wedding feast
Without me no placating of the gods
Whereas the goat
What is he worth

4: Said the goat
My sagacity is unrivalled
You can see it from my beard
It is longer
than the beard of any mandarin

3: Said I to the animals
Stop
disputing each other's worth
Each has his own particular gifts
Respect one another
Do the best you can
each in his own way

Live together in peace
>[*3, 4, 5 turn towards the court group in N.*]

5: The emperor there
plans to build himself a palace
with a hundred roofs

4: From the imperial park
we hear singing and the sound of flutes
>[*Music begins. 3 parodies Chinese poetry.*]

3: On his artificial lake
in a lacquered boat
among naked serving girls
listening
the Emperor
Le Tuong
>>[*9 as emperor falls to the ground. A scream. Music ends.*]

10: A mandarin has stabbed the emperor
>>[*Violent dispersal of both groups in N and S. 9, 10, 11 as group of Nguyen princes in S. 7, 8 as group of Trinh princes in N. Between them 1, 2, 3, 4, 5, 6 as Viet Nam people, widely separated from one another.*]

5: Now the princes of Viet Nam
are fighting for the throne

9, 10, 11: In the south of Viet Nam
power lies
with the princes Nguyen

7, 8: In the north of Viet Nam
the princes Trinh are raising armies
against the Nguyen
>>[*12, 13 as Dutch sailors from SE to Trinh group in N. 12, 13 dressed in white. 12 bears a Dutch emblem of rank. 13 carries a sword and a broad-brimmed hat. After them 14, 15 as Portuguese sailors from SW to Nguyen group in S. 14, 15 dressed*]

in white. 14 with a Portuguese emblem of
rank. 15 with sword and admiral's hat of
eighteenth century. Simultaneously cere-
monial greeting between Trinh and
Dutch, Nguyen and Portuguese.]

14: We bring you greetings
    from the royal government in Lisbon
    and offer you help
    in your righteous war

12: We bring you greetings
    from the royal government in Amsterdam
    and are ready to help you

15: We will build arms factories
    and instruct you in modern warfare

13: We offer you our best weapons
    and put military advisers at your disposal

 8: We accept your help
    In return you shall have cloves
    nutmeg and pepper
    as you request

12: The weapons must of course
    be paid for in pearls and silver

10: We gratefully accept your support
    In return we give you rice
    tea and hardwood
    as you request

14: The arms factories must of course
    be paid for in gold

        [Following the ceremony 12 as Dutch-
        man goes to NW and 13 as Dutchman
        to NE. At the same time 14 as Portuguese
        goes to SW and 15 as Portuguese to SE.
        They watch events from these corners of
        the stage. 7, 8 as Trinh princes and 9, 10,
        11 as Nguyen princes go to the group of
        peasants to recruit soldiers.]

 7: You may keep one son

to work in the fields
The other sons must come with me
9: All who hide
or try to run away
will be hanged
8: March with the Trinh army
against the enemy in the south
10: Help the Nguyen princes
in their fight
for the unity of Viet Nam
11: The fishermen to the galleys
Lash them to the oars
> [*Evasive action and resistance from the
> peasants. Start of flight movement in di-
> rection W.*]
1: We killed a recruiting officer
So they burned down our village
3: We are fleeing to the mountains
11: Women and children to fetch stones
to strengthen the border
against the Trinh
4: The mercenaries
have slaughtered my buffalo
2: The collectors
have taken away the harvest
> [*3 on raised platform in W. He turns to
> the still hesitant peasants.*]
3: They take away your cattle and your land
then drag you off to their armies
the Trinh in the north
and the Nguyen in the south
You will be made to fight for them
against each other
4: We don't want to make the landlords
fatter still
3: You can't even feed yourselves
from your work

But the wealthy
buy themselves offices and honours
[*1 on raised platform in* W.]
1: Bring your cattle to the mountains
Bring as much rice
as you can carry
3: Bring weapons with you
[*The Dutch and Portuguese encourage the
Trinh and Nguyen from their corners.*]
12: Put troops across the roads
15: Seize all wandering peasants
14: Occupy rebellious villages
Arrest the elders
13: Put the agitators' families
on forced labour
[*Of the peasants only 6 still remains in
the centre. Trinh and Nguyen advance
slowly and threateningly on each other.*]
6: The fields dry up
The villages stand empty
We see smoke from the camps
up in the mountains
[*6 also goes to* W.]
4: Sharpen bamboo sticks
for the traps
Hammer out spearheads
2: The game you have killed
will be fairly divided
1: Everything you bring to the mountains
will be used for the common good
[*The Viet Nam peasants, now armed,
from* W *towards Trinh and Nguyen.*]
3: Go down to the plains
The landlords have plenty
Take whatever you need
7, 8, 9,
10, 11: The peasants are coming down from the

                    mountains
                    with a huge army
1, 2, 3,
4, 5, 6: The army of the Tay Son
        1: The peasants are led by three brothers
        6: The brothers Tay Son
1, 2, 3: We shall help ourselves
                    to the things we once carried to the
                    storehouses
                    on our own shoulders
                        [*The Viet Nam peasants drive the Trinh
                        and Nguyen apart.*]
        6: Now the mandarin is frightened of us
        3: Standing there helpless
                    with his long fingernails
                    and his venerable beard
2, 3, 5: All we have brought up
                    from the valleys
                    will be fairly divided
                        [*Music starts.*]
        5: Whirlwinds and storms
                    in the year of the tortoise
        6: The rivers overflow their banks
                        [*Music ends. The Dutch and Portuguese,
                        12, 13, 14, 15 move backwards in defen-
                        sive attitudes.*]
        2: The Dutch flagship
                    is leaving Hai Phong
        3: The Portuguese traders
                    hurry off in their ships
1, 2, 3: The armed peasants
                    come back to their villages
4, 5, 6: The armed peasants
                    are guarding the fields
                    on the Red River
                    and the Mekong
1, 2, 3,

4, 5, 6: The victorious armies of the Tay Son
          march into Saigon and Hanoi
          [*9, 10, 11 as Nguyen princes retreat to SE*
          and remain there in bowed positions. 7,
          8 lay down the Trinh emblems and join
          the group of armed peasants. 1, 2, 3, 4, 5,
          6, 7, 8 as Viet Nam people form a long
          extended row at centre. From this 1, 2, 3,
          5 come forward as chorus.]

CHORUS: With the brothers Tay Son
          the peasant army marched out
          to put an end
          to injustice
          They helped themselves
          from the landlords' stores
          What they took
          they divided fairly
          [*1, 2, 3, 5 return to the row. 7, 8 are given*
          helmets by assistants A and B. Music
          starts.]

1, 2, 3: After the defeat of the Trinh princes
          and the Nguyen princes

4, 5, 6: After the restoration
          of unity
          in the land of Viet Nam

7, 8: We
          the brothers Tay Son
          proclaim one of ourselves
          emperor
          [*8 is dressed in the imperial robes. Music*
          ends.]

8: A new era begins
          under the just rule
          of the Emperor Hue
          [*The row disperses.*]

1, 4, 5: We heard
          a new era is beginning

8: The emperor's brothers
   are taking over
   the administration of the state
2: Then we shall get our reward
   for fighting
1: They will give us our share
   of all the fields
6: They will give us seeds
5: We shall have cattle and tools
3: Our sons will return
   and help us in the fields
7: I command the army
   to enforce
   the decision of the government
   The commandants will supervise
   the distribution of land
   and the collection of taxes
   Their troops are instructed
   to use force
   to quell all resistance
   I order every peasant
   to surrender his weapons

   [7, 8 *as brothers Tay Son retire to raised
   level N. Assistants A and B collect the
   weapons from the peasants and take them
   to the Tay Son. The group of Nguyen 9,
   10, 11 in SE straighten up slowly. The
   peasant group withdraws to N and sits
   down below the Tay Son brothers.*]

PHASE V

[13, 14 *as delegates of the French king come
from SW across front in direction SE to the
Nguyen group. 13, 14 dressed in white. 13
with coat of arms of Louis XVI. 14 with*

sword. *Both are wearing white wigs.* 10 *as*
Nguyen Anh goes to meet them. 10 *in man-*
darin's robe. Ceremonial greeting between
French and Nguyen.]

13: The delegates of the court of Versailles
bring to Prince Nguyen
a message from his gracious majesty
King Louis the Sixteenth

14: His Majesty was much pleased
with your young prince Ming Mang
who was presented to His Majesty
by the Bishop of Behaine

13: The court was ravished
by the prince's noble character
and the charm of his manners

14: His Majesty has decided
to help Prince Nguyen Anh
to attain the position
which is his due

13: It is France's conviction
that only the leadership of Nguyen Anh
can restore peace
to your unhappy country

10: We accept your offer
with deep gratitude
With the support of your troops
our lawful dynasty will easily
achieve its object
Our loyal supporters
within the army and administration of the
    Tay Son
are ready for the call
which will enable them
to throw off the chains of tyranny

13: France can immediately send ashore
twelve hundred infantrymen
two hundred bombardiers

                two hundred and fifty native soldiers
                from our possessions in India
        10: The house of Nguyen
                gives to France
                in recognition of its generous services
                the island of Poulo Condore and also
                control over the port of Da Nang
        14: The court of Versailles stipulates
                that in return for its aid
                France shall be given exclusive trading rights
                within your realm
                        [*Ceremony of mutual agreement. The
                        group of people moves slowly away from
                        the Tay Son in direction S to centre.*]

         3: Once
                the Tay Son used to share out
                what we had won
                fairly
        1, 2: We used once to praise
                the Tay Son for their leadership
                when we fought together with them
                against the bosses
        4, 5: Remember
                when the Tay Son called on us
                to storm the bosses in their strongholds
         3: Now the treasuries and storehouses
                of their own bosses fill up
                while they look on
                        [*In a swift movement the Nguyen and
                        the French take over the positions of the
                        Tay Son on the raised level N. 8 as em-
                        peror lies stretched out in front of the
                        raised level. 7 goes over to the Nguyen
                        group.*]
         9: In a naval battle off Qui Nhon
                we overcame
                the Tay Son fleet

11: We have taken Hanoi

 7: The mandarins and landowners
   swear undying loyalty
   to Prince Nguyen Anh

10: With the help of our mighty French allies
    we have broken
    the shameful rule of the Tay Son

> *[Farewell ceremony between Nguyen and the French. The French go off in NE, followed by 11 from Nguyen group. The people stand wide apart at centre. Music begins.]*

1: Tay Son lies in the gutter

2: Soldiers piss on the Emperor Hue

4: They have seized his son

6: They bring in four elephants

2: Bind him between them

1: They drive the elephants apart

5: The elephants tear him in pieces

6: Then the ravens come

> *[1, 2, 3, 4, 5, 6 stay in position and form a chorus.]*

CHORUS: Do you hear the flocks of ravens
    Do you hear the flocks of ravens
    over the river and over the plain
    Do you hear the cries of the ravens
    Do you hear the cries of the ravens
    on the fields of the plains
    Do you see the flocks of ravens
    The ravens are eating the dead

> *[Music ends. 8 gets up, lays the imperial insignia aside and joins the group of Viet Nam people.]*

PHASE VI

[13, 14 *as delegates of Napoleon come from
SW to N towards the Nguyen, consisting of
7, 9, 10. 13, 14 dressed in white, with a few
embellishments characteristic of Napoleonic
times. Laconic style of speech as they walk
past the people.*]

13: Remarkable
how easily the mob can be stirred up
to rebellion even here
One only needs to preach something about
    equality
and hint at the prospect of booty
and at once everybody is agog
to beat up his master

14: And how senseless all this bloodshed is
when the people's tribunes here
are just as incapable as ours
of running the state

13: What they need is a ruler
with the will and imagination
to build on the ruins of revolution
and restore the country
to its former greatness
        [*Ceremonial greetings between French
        delegates and Nguyen.*]

10: We have heard of the victories
of your great Napoleon
and of your aim
to restore peace in Europe
We wish the alliance with your mighty
    empire
to benefit our own people

14: A new golden age

shall dawn in this land

10: We lay aside
our princely name of Nguyen Anh
and assume the rank
more fitted to our high endeavours
   [*Assistants A and B wrap the imperial
   robe around him. Music begins. 13, 14
   as French delegates remain beside the
   Nguyen.*]

7, 9, 13, 14: The era
of change
is dawning
   [*Music ends. 1, 2, 3, 4, 5, 6, 8 as people
   of Viet Nam still widely separated in statuesque attitudes.*]

8: We hear something about changes

6: We hear
the emperor is calling himself
Gia Long

10: I proclaim that Chinese is no longer
the official language
From now on we shall use
the European script

4: What's the good of that to me
I can't read it either

9: Schools will be open to all

5: Who can pay the teachers

9: Public office is open to all

3: Who can buy themselves a job

7: Only an elite can govern the state

10: Then let the eldest sons
of the mandarins
be educated free

14: To maintain order in the new state
we propose the introduction
of new laws

1: We're told
   the new statute book
   runs to twenty-two volumes
7: The mandarins will be paid
   in harvest produce and silver
9: In return for their loyalty and devotion
   the emperor grants them
   estates and villages
   to use for their own profit
        [*The French delegates start on a tour
        reminiscent of the earlier tours of the
        mandarins. 7, 9, 10 remain in N as im-
        perial court.*]
13: The harbour in Saigon is too small
    for our ships
    We must build new quays and fortresses
14: We will make Saigon
    the centre of Asian trade
 1: What's that we hear
    Trade
    What's in it for us
13: We will build mines
    improve the rice production
    lay new roads
 4: They're after us again
 2: New roads
    to get our harvests to them
    quicker
 3: So their troops can move about
    quicker
10: In Tonking we shall produce
    saltpetre and lead
 5: They're fetching men and children
    from the fields
    and sending them down the mines
        [*2, 8 walk towards E and represent miners*

in front of the raised level. Music starts.]

2: We are down in the mine shaft
8: Don't know if it's day or night
2: Working on our backs
   hacking the rock with pickaxes
8: When the baskets are full
   children drag them to the rope
2: Once a day they let down a basket
   with a bowl of rice
8: Working on our backs
   sleeping in the rubble
2: Not knowing
   if weeks have gone by
   or months

> [*End of music. The French delegates go
> off in NE. 1, 2, 3, 4, 5, 6, 7, 8, 9, 10 as
> Viet Nam people—9, 10 as members of
> the upper class—form an irregular circle
> at centre. 12, 15 as French colonists come
> from SW to make a slow tour among the
> people. 12, 15 dressed in white and wear-
> ing embellishments characteristic of the
> late nineteenth century.*]

15: What splendid prospects
    for an enterprising man
    In no time at all
    I've got myself set up for life
    Safest places to invest in
    are the delta areas of the Mekong
    and the Red River in the north
12: Plenty of natural harbours along the coast
    Towns close to the sea
    Excellent conditions for trade
15: The large rivers make transport easy
    from the interior to the ports
12: In Cochin China alone

there are two million workers
keen and unassuming
15: Cochin China
lies at the very gates of China
From Saigon we can exert strong control
over the Asian trade
12: Here in Cochin China
we can catch up
on Britain's lead

> [*12 looks through a telescope in direction
> SW. 11, 13 appear there as British colo-
> nists, dressed in white. 11 with topee, 13
> with officer's cap of the late nineteenth
> century. Assistants A and B follow them,
> each with British emblems. A and B
> dressed in white. 11 with telescope looks
> in direction S. They move slowly in di-
> rection SE.*]

11: No foggy towns
no discontented workers
no threats of strikes no savage competition
here in India Burma Malaya China
Just vast areas of land waiting
for us to exploit them
13: This is the way to free our kingdom
from poverty and unemployment
The surplus population
can be absorbed
Industry gains
new markets
11: It's as I always said
Empire is a matter of the stomach
If we want to avoid civil war
we must become imperialists

> [*The British colonists 11, 13 go off with
> assistants A and B in SE. The people of*

*Viet Nam as before at centre. The French
colonists 12, 15 armed and in aggressive
attitudes.*]

12: White devils
   they call us
   We must deal most severely
   with this aggression
   of which we hear so much

15: We must protect
   our missionaries

12: In Tonking our brothers
   are being compelled by torture
   to renounce
   their Christian faith

15: Shut up in cages
   Put in chains
   Thrown in boiling oil

12: We can raise soldiers in Cochin China
   Renowned for their courage they will prove
   unbeatable when trained
   in European tactics

12, 15: All civilised nations
   will applaud us
   when we avenge
   these atrocities

   [*Loud music begins, reminiscent of gun
   salvoes. 14 comes from SE as a French
   admiral, with drawn sword. Behind him
   comes assistant A with a French emblem.
   Both come forward to centre.*]

12, 15: The cruisers *Gloire* and *Victorieuse*
   enter the harbour of Da Nang

14: The ships' guns
   have blasted the fortresses to pieces
   An expeditionary force now occupies the
      town

   [*11 from SE as a French admiral, with*

drawn sword. Behind him comes assistant
B with a French emblem. Both forward
to centre.]

12, 15: The flagship *Nemesis*
enters the port of Saigon

11: The forts have been silenced
Our troops move on
into the interior

[*13 comes from SE as an American ad-*
miral, with raised American emblem, to
centre.]

13: The gunboat *Constitution*
of the United States of America
comes to the aid of France

[*Music ends. 9, 10 as members of the up-*
per classes come forward from the group
of Viet Nam people. Opposite them the
colonists in a half circle.]

10: The government of Viet Nam undertakes
to shape its foreign policy
in close conformity with France

12: France for its part promises
to maintain law and order
by stationing troops inside the country

[*The group of people moves slowly in di-*
rection N. 9, 10 remain in front of the
colonists.]

2: After a day in the fields
we go to work in the stone quarries

1: Dragging out the hewn boulders

[*Music starts. 1, 2, 3, 4, 5, 6, 7, 8 form a*
chorus.]

CHORUS: Along the deep ravine
we drag the boulders
Across the mountains
we drag the boulders
Along the deep ravine

across the mountains
the gang leader's shout
pursues us
  [*Music ends.*]
15: France promises
  to hold troops in readiness
  to defend the land
  from outside attack
9: The government of Viet Nam undertakes
  to surrender no territory to foreign powers
  without France's consent
    [*Music starts. Chorus of the people.*]
CHORUS: Our hate goes deeper
  than the ravine
  Our anger rises higher
  than the mountains
  From the deep ravine
  across the mountains
  our shout rings out
  Freedom
    [*The group of people remains in N. 9, 10
    also withdraw in direction N. Assistants
    A and B go off with the emblems.*]

PHASE VII

  [*11, 12, 13, 14, 15 as French colonists in a
  half-circle open to S. The composition of the
  group is reminiscent of the grouping for the
  animal fable earlier. Operatic style of delivery.*]
13: In the contest of the great nations
  to exploit the riches of the earth
  France has won an unbreakable hold
  in the south-east of Asia
14: To ensure the highest profits
  from produce so cheaply obtained

transport to the markets of Europe
must be inexpensive and fast
11: The junks and sampans of the Mekong
    delta
    must be at our merchants' command
    Produce to be brought to loading points
    for forwarding to Saigon
12: The Mekong should be made negotiable to
    Yunnan
    Then from Saigon we could control
    the entire West China trade
    and make things difficult for Britain
13: Via the Mekong we have reached the lake
    of Tonle Sap
    and there in the jungle discovered mythical
    Angkor
    So once more France presents the world
    with the relics of an ancient culture
14: Our gunboats have penetrated further north
    firing salvoes in the thickets on the banks
    But the Mekong provides no passage to
    China
    only to the mountains of Laos
15: In the north the Red River led us
    through the plains of Tonking to Yunnan
    We brought a load of salt
    and heavy weapons to Man Hao
11: The mandarins are blocking the river route
    with the help of outdated treaties
    They say we can trade only in the south
    and obstruct development in Tonking
14: Since the economy cannot expand
    without the products and labour of Tonking
    let us throw out the mandarins of Hanoi
    and hoist our flag on the citadel
         [11, 12, 13, 14, 15 *move closer together
         and form a chorus. Music begins.*]

CHORUS: In the name of progress and peace
we declare the Red River
open to international trade
under the protection of France
[*The French colonists station themselves
in a long row from SE to NE. 9, 10 join
them. 1, 2, 3, 4, 5, 6, 7, 8 as Viet Nam
peasants form a long row from NW to
SW opposite the colonists.*]

15: To counter the threat
to our settlements and
mission stations
the district chief proclaims

12: From the onset of darkness
no one may enter or leave the village
without permission

13: All found in possession of weapons
will receive one hundred strokes of the cane
and two years' imprisonment

4: The traders force us
to sell our harvests
cheap

6: Then they sell the rice we need
for much more than they gave

11: Peasants who cannot maintain their families
can find work in the tin mines of Tonking

15: Those not required in the mines
can apply for work
in the rubber plantations of An Nam

3: And if you don't get in there
they put you in the army

2: Or you go off to the mountains

4: I have sown
right up to the door of my hut
But still I can't grow enough
to feed my family

[*10 comes forward and goes to the peasants.*]

10: Pawn your buffalo with me
For the money
I'll rent you
a bit of land

8: I spun these ropes
with hemp

10: I've no use for your ropes
any more
They make cheaper ropes
in France

8: Then I must ask
for time to pay

10: I can't wait any longer
I'll have to take
some of your land
[*The speakers of the following indicate 10.*]

1: The biggest part of our work
goes into *his* pocket

2: We rent our land
from *him*

4: We pay *him*
taxes

5: From *him*
we borrow money

7: And *he*
gets the land
when we can't pay
the interest
[*The row of peasants splits up into four variously spaced pairs at centre. The colonists and their Vietnamese allies 9, 10 remain in close formation in E.*]

3: Many of our people have left the village

They are in the mountains
We are collecting weapons
to use against *him*

11: We are putting in soldiers
to crush the terrorist groups

12: We seize all wandering vagabonds
and put them to forced labour

1, 6: There are five thousand of us
on a coffee plantation
near Pleiku
We work from dawn
to darkness
Nobody helps the sick
We bury our dead
before we start for work

2, 5: We are clearing the jungle
in the valley of Bien Hoa
for the firm of Michelin
to make new rubber plantations

3, 7: We are laying a railway
from Dalat down to the port of Phan Rang
Transport route for cotton and tea

4, 8: We have been conscripted
for work in the anthracite mines
of Hon Gay

11: The mining company of Tonking
has exported more than five hundred
thousand tons
of coal this year

12: The Portland Cement Company at Hai
Phong
records a seventy per cent
rise in profits

13: In Cai Bau and Dong Trieu
we have opened up mines
for the extraction of zinc lead and
manganese

14: The grocers in the motherland
    have received a million tons of rice
    from Indochina
    to sell this season
15: France holds the exclusive
    trading rights with Indochina
    France determines
    the selling prices
 8: I can't pay my rent for the field any longer
13: Exports this season
    one million two hundred thousand tons of
        rice
 1: We can earn a few coppers
    in the warehouses on the quay
 7: And buy a bit of brandy or opium
12: Our monopoly
    of opium and alcohol
    brings in a good
    and secure profit
13: Opium and alcohol
    also serve
    to keep the natives
    quiet
 5: A few families
    own most of the cultivated land
    on the Mekong
    A lot of families sweat
    to maintain their rented field
    The families that lose
    their last bit of land
    are countless
14: Before the turn of the century
    the Bank of Indochina
    handled two hundred million
    In little more than ten years that rose
    to a thousand million
15: The Bank of Indochina makes sure

          that credits for industrial projects
do not fall into the hands
of Vietnamese employers
Thus we prevent the emergence
of competition

3: They cover their coats of arms with their
      slogan
Liberty Equality Fraternity
But in the factories the white worker
gets much more than we earn

2: Many children die
shortly after birth

3: Forty-five in every thousand

1: No food
no medical aid
for the weak and the sick

9, 10: Particular care must be taken to ensure
that no groups are formed among the
      workers
on plantations and in factories
Every hint of political activity
or any other sign of rebellion
and moral degradation
must be rigorously stamped out

4: Tomorrow when darkness falls
we'll meet behind the store

8: Escaping back
to the villages

        [*The group of people goes to W and re-
        mains there, part on the platform. 9, 10,
        11, 12, 13, 14, 15 go to NE. There 12 and
        13 receive steel helmets and rifles from as-
        sistants A and B. 9, 10, 12, 13 go off in
        NW. 14, 15 remain as French soldiers in
        NE.*]

PHASE VIII

[*Short pause without movement.*]
4: We're told
   that war has broken out
   in Europe
14: The war has been
   forced on France
15: France needs more workers and more
      soldiers
14: All able-bodied people must be mobilised
   to withstand the German attack
15: Fifty thousand workers
   are needed at once
   to build fortifications
14: And fifty thousand men
   to reinforce the army
      [*The French soldiers go off in NE. 9, 10
      dressed in black, come from NW to
      group of people. 1, 2, 3, 4, 5, 6, 7, 8, 9,
      10 as people of Viet Nam start slow
      movement forward to centre.*]
4: We're told
   the war is over
6: Have the French won
10: They have killed
   millions of enemy soldiers
3: France too
   has lost millions of soldiers
6: They must be vast countries
   to have such large armies
9: We were there
   at the front
   We killed a lot of white soldiers

4: Why did you help them
   in their war
9: We had no work
   Our families were starving
   We needed the pay
5: Many of those who were sent to Europe
   have not returned
8: What were they fighting for
1: Roads and rivers
   mines and factories
3: They fought to extend
   their boundaries
7: And what did France gain by it
2: France gained land from the enemy
   The enemy has to pay large tributes
3: The enemy has to give up its colonies
   and hand over its fleet
6: And what reward do you get
   for helping France
   to beat the enemy
9: We are still not allowed
   to become officers
   We are still
   getting the lowest rate of pay
4: What are the soldiers in France getting
   for winning the war
   Does every soldier in France
   get his bit of land
1: Most of the soldiers are going
   into factories and workshops
3: There are a lot of factories in France
1: They are building ships
   motor cars and airplanes
7: Now that France has won
   will we be better paid
   in the mines and plantations
8: Will we get the right

       they have in France
       to elect our own representatives
10: We are told
       we are colonials
       Only French citizens have the right
       to choose their representatives
 4: Some sailors told us
       in Europe the workers
       combine to form unions
 3: In France they stop working
       when the factory owner refuses
       to pay higher wages
       They march in thousands through the
          streets
 2: But the factory owner puts the police on to
          them
       They beat up the workers
       Sometimes they even shoot
 4: The sailors told us about a country
       where the workers have seized power
 3: This land is called Russia
       At first people refused
       to work in the arms factories
       Their soldiers stopped
       obeying their officers
       The peasants stopped
       delivering corn to the army
       The railwaymen went on strike
 1: Then they forced their way into the
          emperor's palace
       They shot the emperor and all his lackeys
 3: In Russia the workers
       have driven out the factory owners
       and the peasants have shared the
          landowners' estates
       among themselves
 7: If we go in great numbers

to the factory owner's house
he is bound to give way to our demands

2: In France the factory owners promise
the workers improvements
They say improvements will come
when the workers have increased their
production

1: They say
they need timber
coal rubber metals
for their factories

8: The foremen will not give us our pay
They say we owe them money
for food and lodging

7: Food
mouldy rice

4: Lodging
the bare earth

5: Let's go to the factory owner's house

1: To the plantation office

4: To the governor's house

5: We will take our children along
and show the governor
that they are hungry

3: Do you think
they will listen to you
They will tell you
to go back to work

7: We can't work
if we don't eat

3: They'll give you nothing

2: They will seize some of you
and throw you in prison

1, 4, 5: We will wait

3: They'll shoot at you

[*1, 2, 3, 5 come together to form a chorus.
Music starts.*]

CHORUS: Again and again they rose up
        against enemies who invaded the country
        and against oppressors in their own land
        They drove out the foreigners
        threw down their own masters
        But in fighting the one
        they delivered themselves to the other
        All that changed in thousands of years were
        the names of the rulers
    5: They are the force
        that every invader crushed
        They are the force
        on which each dynasty
        based its power
    2: For thousands of years they bore the
            oppression
        seeking their liberty in rebellion
        And liberty meant for them
        freedom from debt and more land to plough
        And this each new leader promised them
    1: But first the leaders gave land
        to their own families
        and to their followers
        And these demanded more and more land
        So less and less land remained
        for the peasants
CHORUS: And so they revolted again
        and new leaders came to their head
        But the peasants could never remove
        the causes of their oppression
    3: Now no leader can ever
        promise the peasants land
        for France alone
        decides how the soil
        shall be divided
CHORUS: Now is the time for learning
        Russia was backward

the peasants enslaved
the number of revolutionaries small
the workers inexperienced
and uneducated
But their passion and their courage were
  great
And so they established their rule
  [*Music ends.*]

PHASE IX

[1, 2, 3, 4, 5, 6, 7, 8, 9, 10 *as cadre of the rev-*
olutionary underground organisation in Viet
Nam come forward in direction S. The group
comes to a standstill facing S, in a wide half
circle, with 1, 2, 3 in the middle. The arrange-
ment is reminiscent of the animal fable scene.]
1: Directives say
   that workers in the developed countries
   must establish close contact
   with liberation movements in the colonies
   They say
   national and colonial oppression
   can be overcome
   only by joint effort
   The struggle at home
   must be subordinated
   to the progress of the struggle
   in all other countries
   But here
   at this moment
   we cannot count
   on help
   from the workers of Europe
4: The workers in France
   look on us as inferior beings

incapable of thought and action
They think of the colonies
as sundrenched deserts or
lands of green coconut palms
They know no better and so
are not interested
in the liberation of the colonies
Far from identifying themselves with us
they stand firm
behind their bourgeois governments

2: Meanwhile the bosses are putting more
        pressure
    on the workers in France
    trying to save themselves from bankruptcy
    now they've let America get the upper hand
    France owes the United States more than
        half
    its whole national assets

7: So they'll squeeze the colonies
    more ruthlessly than ever
    Starvation wages for us

1: But we will show them
    that the proletariat of a backward colonial
        country
    can seize power more easily
    than in the developed countries of the West

4: There are dispossessed peasants enough
    in the plantations
    an army of workers
    in the mines factories and harbours
    They'll soon learn
    how to fight

3: But we can't set up councils
    of workers and peasants
    until the people understand
    what it's all about
    We face a difficult task

How to dispel ignorance
Many people in our country
know no other condition but slavery
2: So far it's the educated middle classes
who have resisted most
We must get the most progressive of them
on our side
The policy of our party
must be a national one
appealing to all
who want to see colonialism
destroyed
4: We know what will happen
if the middle class
is given its head
The democratic citizens of France
preach equality too
but at the same time say
private property is sacred
2: If our revolution
looks bourgeois to start with
that doesn't mean
we have given in
to the bourgeoisie
It simply means
we use the privileges of the middle classes
to benefit the whole people
We must be careful
not to push them aside
or we shall drive them
into the arms of the counter-revolution
4: Our party
is the party of the oppressed
and the enslaved
Our struggle here
in the backward countries
will decide

whether revolution
can be brought back
to the international plane
3: Our resistance
is a resistance of the whole people
Everyone
of whatever social class
must be mobilised and armed
We need the teachers and the students
We need all who can read and write
all who have carts and oxen
and full larders
We need the people
who know how to organise
who can manage technical teams
who are experienced in military ways
1: But the first job of our cadre
is to win the confidence of the villagers
You know how they look on strangers
And who can blame them
All they know are people
who come to plunder
destroy and burn
Never forget
that these are the ones
who one day will smash down oppression
Your job is simply
to open their eyes
5: We have learnt
when we go to the villages
to listen
Not to explain
until they ask
We help them in their work
look after the sick
teach them to read and write
7: We bring them what they need

Knives salt needles pencils paper
When we have lived with them a while
we start with hygienic improvements

8: We try to cure them
of superstition

6: We tell them
the history of our country
About the peasants' risings

9: This will give them confidence
in their own strength

10: They will begin
to grasp the meaning
of political demands

6: And understand that many others
are making the same demands

10: And that to get what they demand
they must fight
with arms

[*The group remains a few moments motionless.*]

PHASE X

[*14, 15 come as French soldiers from NW to centre. 14, 15 dressed in white, with steel helmets and machine guns.*]

14: Germany is threatening
its neighbour countries
Italy is fighting
in Africa
Japan
seeking domination in Asia
has occupied
large parts of China

15: The Front Populaire government of France

is sending out a commission
to find out how
the native population
can be won
for the defense of Indochina
14: We count on Indochina's loyalty
in this hour of trial
> [*The French soldiers separate and move
> to the platforms W and E, where they
> remain watching. 1, 2, 3, 4, 5, 6, 7, 8, 9,
> 10 move apart in a single movement. 4,
> 5, 6, 7, 8, 9, 10 as people of Viet Nam
> move slowly to centre and position them-
> selves at wide intervals. 1, 2, 3 as mem-
> bers of the liberation movement remain
> in S.*]

1: The commission is calling for reports
on conditions in the country
2: Now we can hold meetings
in the villages
legally
3: The people are encouraged to speak openly
> [*1, 2, 3, move to centre.*]
3: You have the right
to complain
8: We know what will happen
if we complain
Get out
5: Let them speak
and tell us
what they want
3: You must talk plainly
about the way you live
They want to put an end
to injustices
9: We are hungry

You know that already

1: Yet you carry your harvests with your own
   hands
   to the landlords

8: Get out of sight
   before they grab you

3: The soldiers over there
   won't shoot

2: Meetings are being held
   in other villages too

6: Why aren't the soldiers shooting now

3: There's a new government in France
   which won't allow its soldiers
   to shoot at us

10: There's a war coming
    They want us to defend the country

8: Is that why you're here
   To fetch us for the army

1: If an army is raised
   it won't be to fight for France

6: Quiet
   The soldiers might hear you

7: Where do you come from
   Who are you

3: We speak for many workers in the towns
   for many labourers on the plantations
   and for soldiers too

2: We have joined together
   in a large group

5: Then can you help us
   to keep our harvests

4: Can you give us oxen

3: First you must set up a council in the
   village
   and discuss together
   what should be changed

5: We get nothing from our earnings

The taxes take it all
7: Salt taxes
   Ground rents
   Compulsory loans
1: But you know who collects the taxes
   You know who pockets it all
9: We'll kill him
2: Protest
   Find out
   what's happening in other villages
1: The new government in France
   has sent a commission
   to listen to your complaints
2: Tell the commission
   how many hours a day you have to work
   Tell them
   who it is you work for
   Tell them too
   about the extra work the women have to do
6: You mean the women
   can complain too
3: Men and women must
   have equal rights
9: We need a school
5: The neighbouring villages
   have no schools either
   If every village asks for a school
   will we get teachers
1: Teachers will be sent
   to all villages no matter how remote
   if all of you demand it
8: If we set up a council
   will we get land as well
3: The people who have got the land now
   will never give it up
   voluntarily
10: You mean

we must use force
3: There is no other way than force
to put an end to injustices
2: Everyone will get as much land
as he can cultivate
The councils must supervise
the distribution
4: Will every village
have these councils
1: There will be councils in all the villages
The workers will form councils too
in the factories
4: But can the workers
run the factories
3: That is our goal
All factories
mines and plantations
shall become the property
of the workers

> [*Loud music begins.* 12, 13 *as Japanese
> soldiers come from NW and NE, dressed
> in white. Both carry Japanese emblems.
> Assistants A and B accompany them. A
> and B dressed in white. The French sol-
> diers* 14, 15 *hand over their weapons to
> assistants A and B.* 1, 2, 3, 4, 5, 6, 7, 8, 9,
> 10 *as people of Viet Nam form a group
> of several rows at centre.* 1, 2, 3, *in the
> front row.*]

5: In all harbours
on all roads
7, 8: All airports and railways
6, 9, 10: Japanese troops
4, 5, 6,
9, 10: Japanese troops
in every town
1: On France's roads

in France's towns
German troops
14: The Japanese troops have been given the
    right
to use our territory
for assembly areas
15: The Governor General has surrendered the
    country
to the occupying power
14: Thus saving forty thousand French citizens
from internment
12, 13: All resistance
will be punished by death
    [*The French soldiers, followed by assis-*
    tants A and B, go off in NW and NE.
    Music ends.]
1: At village assemblies and in the market
    places
2: At secret meetings in the cities
1: This letter is being read
    [*3 comes forward to S. The group stands*
    motionless behind him.]
3: You see them still
the French masters in our country
You see them in their uniforms
They still have rifles
Their guns still stand
But they have no ammunition
Airplanes they have
but no fuel
They are still there
the French masters
in the banks and offices
But look how cautious
how circumspect they now are
Look how they obey
the new masters in the land

Then look at them
the new masters
They have bullets for their guns
and fuel for their planes
But do not think
that will save them
They have enemies still stronger
than themselves
In China they can go no farther
Britain and America will never yield
their markets here to them
But these great powers
have enemies now in Europe
whom they must crush as well
Now
as they fight each other
for new and old possessions
our time has come
Do as the Chinese people have done
Prepare for the great revolt

> [*In a single violent movement the group
> of people radiates out in all directions.
> Only 1, 2 remain in the centre. 3 rejoins
> them at the same time.*]

1: In every village
you must form groups to defend yourselves
When the Japanese invade your village
and arrest your people
then you must beat the drums

2: You must try
to hold the enemy
till help comes
from the villages nearby

> [*4 goes quickly to 1, 2, 3 at centre.*]

4: We have only one rifle in our village

2: Use clubs

        spears and stakes
        Lay traps
        Dig pits
        Lure soldiers into ambushes
        Kill them
        and seize their weapons
            [4 back to his former place. At the same
            time 6, 9 to centre. Assistants A and B
            with weapons, which they distribute.]
   9: Thousands are starving
       in our province
   3: Then march
       with the people of the neighbouring villages
       to the nearest garrison
       When you've got a few hundreds together
       take the storehouses by surprise
   2: We will be waiting for you there
       and will tell you
       how to open the storehouses
   1: And then you will force them open
   6: But if they shoot at us
   1: You must have an armed squad
       standing behind you
   3: We'll send you soldiers
       from our units
       They will bring weapons
       and plan with you
       how best to attack the enemy
            [6, 9 return to their former places. At the
            same time 4, 7 go to centre.]
   4: We have formed a brigade
       in the province of Bac Can
   7: Many from the villages have joined us
   1: Storm the convoys
   3: Cut off the enemy's reinforcements
       Attack the sentry posts

9: Allow the enemy no rest
[*4, 7 back to their former places. At the same time 6 to centre.*]

6: We have formed a committee
in the province of Lang Son
[*6 back to her former place. At the same time 10 to centre.*]

10: In the factory we are sabotaging
the enemy's supplies
[*10 back to his former place. At the same time 8, 9 to centre.*]

8: Workers in the anthracite mines
are forming a committee

9: Committees in every cotton mill
on every plantation
in every school
[*8, 9 back to their former places. 5 steps forward.*]

5: Committees for each district
[*7 steps forward.*]

7: Committees for each province

3: A committee for the liberation
of the whole country
[*4 steps forward.*]

4: We are getting news
from other villages and provinces
We hear
what methods they are using
[*10 steps forward.*]

10: We are learning
to plan actions over wide distances

3: We know the enemy's movements
throughout the country
[*4, 5, 6, 7, 8, 9, 10 one after another to centre.*]

5: We see
our efforts rewarded

7: A bridge blown up
4: A train ambushed
6: Guns and ammunition captured
8: We are driving out the landlords
5: That means land
   for lots of peasants
3: We are preparing
   to take over the administration
        [*Music begins.*]
4, 5, 7: Whoever cannot fight
   in the Viet Minh army
   supports it
   where he can
6, 8, 9, 10: The Viet Minh army
   is protecting our rights
   Political struggle
   and armed conflict
   are one and
   indivisible
        [*1, 2, 3, 4, 5, 6, 7, 8, 9, 10 form a chorus.*]
CHORUS: To shatter the enemy's strength
   to achieve our independence
   we ourselves must apply
   more strength
        [*Music ends.*]

PHASE XI

3: Officers and soldiers of the freedom army
   attack all towns and centres
   still occupied by the enemy
        [*4, 5, 6, 7, 8, 9, 10 as Viet Minh in wide
        formation to N. The Japanese soldiers in
        NW and NE are disarmed and forced off.
        1, 2, 3 remain at centre. Their words si-
        multaneous with the action.*]

1: Capture railway stations
   post offices
   telephone exchanges
2: Storm police stations
   Free all political prisoners
        [1, 2, 3 *turn in direction S.*]
1: The Viet Minh
   has millions of members
   All who want an independent Viet Nam
   are united in the Viet Minh
   The National Committee for the Liberation
        of Viet Nam
   is our provisional government
2: Japan has surrendered unconditionally
   The Japanese emperor orders his troops
   everywhere
   to lay down their weapons
3: Japan's defeat is not enough
   to give us independence
   The French are trying to regain
   their supremacy
   De Gaulle is negotiating with the Allies
   to appoint a high commissioner
   for Indochina
1: We will get no help
   from Europe
   The partisans in Greece
   who fought the German Fascists
   have been betrayed
   The workers' parties in Italy
   and France
   have given up the fight
   They look on as the great powers
   go on dividing the world
   between them
   Freedom fighters in Indonesia

Malaya Burma and the Philippines
face an unconquerable enemy
Chinese revolutionaries are fighting
Chiang Kai-shek
the ally of the victors in this war
Armies of peasants
come down from the mountains towards the
    towns
The long war
of the robbed and betrayed begins
The war
of the third world

1, 2, 3: When every single one of us is armed
when revolution covers the whole land
then we shall win
> [*Meanwhile the Viet Minh have formed
> themselves into a long row on the raised
> level N. All are armed. 1, 2, 3 turn to
> them.*]

3: Workers peasants mechanics
teachers students
shopkeepers officials
soldiers
Lead our common revolt
to victory

1: In the towns and villages of Viet Nam
in the delta areas and in the mountains
the people's committees
have thrown the mandarins and tycoons
out of office

2: The whole country is in our keeping
> [*The Viet Minh move forward singly and
> irregularly in direction S.*]

4: Political prisoners freed

7: Traitors punished

8: The poll tax abolished

9: Ground rents reduced
6: The quislings' land
confiscated and shared out
5: The Catholic mission estates
divided up
4: Industries taken over
8: The eight-hour working day introduced
9: All citizens are equal before the law
5: Equal rights for men and women
10: Education for all
6: Votes for all
8: Recognition of all democratic rights
[*The Viet Minh group comes to a standstill centre in close formation.* 1, 2, 3 *at
front.*]
1: The chairman of the liberation movement
Ho Chi Minh
has proclaimed on this day
the second of September
nineteen hundred and forty-five
the inauguration of
the Democratic Republic of Viet Nam
3: All men are born equal
and possess from birth
the inviolable right
to life and freedom
Thus it is written in the American
Declaration of Independence
proclaimed in the year
seventeen seventy-six
2: All men are born free
and with equal rights
and thus they shall remain
So it was proclaimed
by the French Revolution
in the year

seventeen eighty-nine
1: With the slogans of their revolution
the French colonial bosses
plundered our land
Their deeds are contrary
to all principles of humanity
and justice
They laid our country waste
and brought misery on our people
3: In autumn nineteen forty
our land ceased to be
a French colony
It became a Japanese colony
When the people took power
in their own hands
we snatched our freedom
from the Japanese
2: The French fled
The Japanese capitulated
The emperor Bao Dai
renounced the throne
Our people abolished
colonial slavery
and created
independent Viet Nam
1: Our people overthrew the monarchy
which had flourished
for thousands of years
and set up in its place
a democratic republic
3: For these reasons we
the members of the provisional government
of the new Viet Nam
representing the whole
Vietnamese people
renounce all connections

with the colonial power of France
and declare all agreements signed by the
    French
 relating to Viet Nam
invalid
All privileges enjoyed by France
in our territory
are now abolished
2: We are confident
that the Allied Powers
who in their conferences
have recognized the principle
of equal rights
for all nations
will also recognise our right
to independence
3: We declare
that Viet Nam has the right
to be free and independent
and that it is now free
and independent
The Vietnamese people is resolved
to do its utmost
to lay down life and property
in order to defend
this right

> *[Sudden appearance of 11 as British sol-
> dier in NW; 12 as Chinese Nationalist in
> NE, accompanied by assistant A with
> Kuomintang emblem; 13 as British sol-
> dier in SW, accompanied by assistant B
> with British emblem; and 14 as American
> soldier in SE. All with national emblems,
> helmets and extended weapons. All are
> dressed in white. Short bursts of music,
> reminiscent of the arrival of the French
> colonial fleet earlier. All advance slowly*

towards the Viet Minh at centre. The
Viet Minh close into a tight group.]

11: In accordance with decisions
made by the Allied governments
British troops have landed
in Indochina

12: Chinese National troops
in the north of Viet Nam

13: We are taking over
the Japanese prisoners of war
and equipping them with weapons

11: We are arming five thousand
French soldiers
released from internment

13: We are occupying
the government buildings in Saigon

14: American ships
are bringing arms and ammunition

11: In preparation for
the return of France
to Indochina

[*15 from SE, dressed in white, with French*
emblem. Delivery slow and solemn.]

15: The cruiser *Gloire*
is now entering
the port of Saigon

PART TWO

PHASE I

[*The side platforms have been placed together at centre front in the form of a square. Similar in appearance to a raised dais on the stage, the construction represents a huge conference table. Around the table at regular intervals are white chairs of the simplest sort. The stage is empty at the start. The participants in the conference, 7, 8, 9, 10, 11, 12, 13, 14, 15, enter, all dressed in white.*]

LOUDSPEAKER: Washington

Third of April

Nineteen hundred and fifty-four

Secret conference

in the Department of State

> [*The participants sit down at the table, 10 at N centre.*]

PROJECTOR: John Foster Dulles

Secretary of State

11: Gentlemen

The President has asked me

to invite you here

to discuss

the alarming situation in Indochina

The President wants Congress

to sanction moves

by our naval and air forces

designed to relieve the French troops

encircled at Dien Bien Phu

PROJECTOR: Admiral Arthur Radford

Chairman of the Joint Chiefs of Staff
12: On the twentieth of March the French
    Head of Staff
General Ely came to see us
He asked for a direct intervention
by us
As you know
France has been fighting for eight years
against the Viet Minh
which grows daily in strength
Following the Navarre Plan
the French built up a stronghold
in the valley of Dien Bien Phu
the intention being to force the enemy
to a decisive battle
However the enemy's strength
was underestimated
Now instead of the planned offensive
a defensive battle must be fought there
PROJECTOR: Roger Kyes
Deputy Secretary of Defense
13: The stronghold is surrounded
and day and night bombarded by enemy
    artillery
from the surrounding heights
The airstrip has been put out of action
12: Since France has all its best troops there
capitulation
would mean a decisive defeat
in the whole of Indochina
11: Gentlemen
France's predicament gives us
compelling reasons to intervene
The spread of Communism
to the countries of Indochina
would be a serious threat
to the free world

PROJECTOR: Senator Eugene Millikin
                        Republican
              9: What economic factors
                        are at stake here
PROJECTOR: Thruston Morton
                        Assistant Secretary of State for
                            Congressional Relations
                        Department of State
            14: The countries of South East Asia
                        have a population of one hundred and
                            sixty-five
                        millions
                        They produce eighty-five per cent of the
                            world's rubber
                        and eighty-two per cent of tin
                        Indochina also possesses
                        high quality anthracite
                        copper and ore as well as so far unexploited
                        stocks of manganese
                        bauxite and tungsten
                        It is the only country in Asia
                        which produces a surplus
                        of rice
                        Whoever controls that
                        holds the whole food supply of Japan
                        India Malaya Java and the Philippines
                        in his hand
                        Indochina's geographical position
                        gives it control of the supply lines
                        between the Pacific and the Indian oceans
            11: The new centre of world Communism
                        is China
                        And China supports the Viet Minh
                        China is out to gain power
                        over the whole of Asia
                        If Viet Nam falls
                        Laos and Cambodia

will also collapse
We should lose
Thailand Burma and Formosa
and be forced back on Hawaii
which would put us back to where we were
before the war

13: Our strategic aim
is to build a chain of bases
around the Russia-China block

> [13, *as Roger Kyes, with a pointer on the
> table. All the others get to their feet, sup-
> port themselves on the table and follow
> Kyes's explanations on the map, which is
> assumed to lie on the table.*]

13: As this map shows
we have already got China covered
from Korea to Viet Nam
In South Korea we have
five hundred thousand men
plus four hundred thousand
loyal South Koreans
In Japan we have
seventy-five thousand men stationed
Allied Japanese troops
one hundred and eighty thousand
On Okinawa
twenty thousand of our own men
Nationalist China's army in Formosa
five hundred thousand men
In Hong Kong
ten thousand British
Our forces in the Philippines
twelve thousand
Allied Filipinos
fifty-seven thousand
British troops in Malaya
one hundred thousand

You see the importance of Indochina
in the line of defense
stretching across Thailand
Pakistan India Iran and Turkey
to Greece
     [13 *returns to his seat. All sit down.*]
14: We must make sure
that revolution Chinese style
does not spread
to these friendly countries
A guerrilla victory in Viet Nam
over a European military power
would put new heart
into rebel movements everywhere
PROJECTOR: Senator William F Knowland
Majority Leader
15: Since nineteen fifty we have been bearing
the main brunt
of the costs of the Indochinese war
Weapons deliveries alone
have cost us
way beyond two thousand million dollars
France must not be allowed
to come to the Geneva conference next
   month
as a defeated nation
We have no wish to defend
Europe's colonial ambitions
On the contrary we are much more
   concerned
to help the Indochinese states
who already have independence within the
   French Union
to complete independence
Only when that's done
will we be able to take over from France
and push our own interests

in Indochina
12: Once the military position
is stabilised
governments willing to work with us
can be set up
PROJECTOR: Senator Richard Russell
Democrat
8: For that we shall need a large number of
ground troops
just as in Korea
Yet we see
France's modern and highly equipped armies
unable to stand up to a militarily much
weaker
but fanatic opponent
PROJECTOR: Senator Earle C Clements
Democrat
7: The Viet Minh are getting heavy guns
and ammunition from China
They have the support
of the majority of the population
Thousands stand ready to bring up supplies
The French have not managed
to break up this provisioning system
12: Conventional weapons
are of little use
in this dense territory
So we've been thinking
of dropping a few small atom bombs
which would work out cheaper
than ground forces
7: How could we justify
the use of atom bombs
11: The deterrent effect on China
is justification enough
7: What do we do if China goes on
sending in weapons

12: Then we shall have to include
    the southern part of China
    in our target area

 7: How explain that
    to world opinion

13: These Chinese arms depots
    are the breeding ground of aggression

12: It would give us a chance to destroy
    those new centres of heavy industry
    on which the Communist government
    bases its prestige

11: It is quite feasible
    gentlemen
    that the threat alone
    would cause the Chinese leaders
    to think again

 7: But if Mao Tse-tung doesn't
    take the hint

12: Then we'll use the atoms
    on Peking

 8: Do you think Russia will stand idly by
    if we get into a fight with China

11: Russia lost twenty million people
    in the last war
    They've enough to do
    rebuilding their own country
    Experience shows
    that the Soviet Union is more interested
    in peaceful solutions

 8: Do the other three Chiefs of Staff
    approve these plans

12: No

 8: Then how can the government
    put forward this project

12: I have spent more time in the Far East
    than anyone else
    and so I know the position best

I shall be able to convince
the General Staff
PROJECTOR: Senator Lyndon B Johnson
Minority Leader
10: Before committing ourselves
to operations in Indochina
we must consult other nations
who might go along with us
Has the Secretary of State done that
11: No
10: Why hasn't the matter been put
to the United Nations
as happened
with the conflict in Korea
Support by UN troops
would demonstrate the legality of our aims
11: There's no time for that
12: Ships of our fleet
have already taken up positions
in the South China Sea
8: Under what formula
13: The aircraft carriers *Essex* and *Philippine
Sea*
have sailed out on routine manoeuvres
7: What is their fighting strength
13: Two hundred fighter planes
some of them equipped with tactical
A-bombs
And B-29 Squadron is standing by
in the Philippines
10: Congress will not be able
to give the requested approval until
our allies have promised their support
We feel public opinion
is not yet ready
to accept the idea of
unilateral action on our part

There is at the moment
no state of emergency
which would justify the President
involving the country in warlike actions
without the approval of Congress
            [*11, 12, 13, remaining in their seats, form
            a chorus. They speak softly, almost whis-
            pering. Meanwhile the others sit motion-
            less. When the chorus ends, the next
            scene begins immediately.*]
CHORUS: But inevitably the day will come
when Congress will grant the President
absolute authority
to take all steps
which he considers vital
for the defense of freedom
LOUDSPEAKER: Washington
Fifth of April
Nineteen fifty-four
President Eisenhower
addresses the nation
over all television networks
            [*10 as* PRESIDENT EISENHOWER *mounts the
            table and comes forward. Assistants A and
            B, coming quickly from SE, place a small
            white rostrum beside him. The others
            lean back in their chairs. The President
            puts on a smile. Loudspeaker in the man-
            ner of a news report, factual in tone.*]
LOUDSPEAKER: Dwight D Eisenhower stands
beside his writing-desk
his right hand resting
on its surface
10: My dear friends I am speaking to you
today on a vital matter I am speaking
about our great nation speaking
about its worries and its problems and

                    about its strength and its future
LOUDSPEAKER: Dwight D Eisenhower sits
                    on the edge of the writing-desk
        10: My dear friends we know
                    we are the most productive nation
                    in the world we know
                    we are wealthier than
                    any other nation
                    on earth we know
                    that militarily we are superior
                    to all other nations why then
                    should we get anxious why
                    should we fear that something
                    might happen to us my friends
LOUDSPEAKER: Dwight D Eisenhower taps
                    his clenched left hand
                    emphatically with the forefinger
                    of his right hand
        10: Our opponent also has
                    the bomb and we must
                    take care that he does not
                    use it against us
                    The world enemy is trying
                    to divide our country he is trying
                    to incite class against class men
                    against men my dear friends
                    You are anxious too about the dangers
                    of depression you have heard
                    that our country has three million
                    seven hundred thousand unemployed
                    This figure has to do with the fact that we
                    are moving from a war economy to
                    an economy of peace and
                    in the process have great adjustments
                    to make my friends
                    the efforts of our nation are directed
                        towards a free

and prospering world
LOUDSPEAKER: Dwight D Eisenhower rises
and clasps his hands together
10: But to make possible this free and
prospering world we must
continue to improve our weapons and
work patiently towards the day when
atom energy will be used exclusively
for peaceful purposes and
contribute to the happiness of all
men women and children
in the world
[*10 returns to his seat. Assistants A and B
carry off the rostrum. The others move.*]
LOUDSPEAKER: Washington
Sixth of April
Nineteen fifty-four
Senate debate
PROJECTOR: Senator William F Knowland
California
[*15 rises.*]
15: We have created the free
and independent republic of the Philippines
We have made possible
the existence of Nationalist China
on Formosa
While we were giving the peoples of Asia
their freedom
the men in the Kremlin were depriving
the peoples of East Europe and the Baltic
of their freedom
Neither these facts nor the sufferings
of the Chinese people
under their imposed rulers
are yet sufficiently appreciated in South East
Asia
We have many good friends in Asia

Syngman Rhee in South Korea
Chiang Kai-shek in Formosa
Ramon Magsaysay in the Philippines
These men should help
to spread the truth
[*15 sits down. 10 rises.*]
PROJECTOR: Senator John F Kennedy
Massachusetts
10: For four years now our experts
have been misjudging
the situation in Indochina
The Secretary of State as well as
the Secretary of Defense and their advisers
have kept on prophesying
a favourable end to the war
In spite of this series of optimistic reports
every member of Congress knows
today there is no prospect of victory
The Geneva talks
will revolve around two main points
Point one
An agreement based on the division of Viet
    Nam
into a Viet Minh zone
and a French Union zone
Point two
A coalition government
in which Ho Chi Minh is represented
For in spite of all wishful thinking
his popularity in Indochina
is a fact
This second solution
must be rejected
In no time at all
the Viet Minh would re-establish its power
over the whole country
I

like Mr Dulles
favour a policy of collective action
But to pour money material and troops
into the jungles of Indochina
too hastily and ineffectively
that would be tantamount to suicide
Only our complete personal commitment
can overcome an enemy who is everywhere
and at the same time nowhere
an enemy which has the sympathies of the
   people
and is supported by the people
Now is the time
for thought and reappraisal
On our decision depends
the peace of the world

PROJECTOR: Senator Mike Mansfield
Montana

8: The Secretary of State
looks to this Congress
for a definite decision
What
in the opinion of the honourable junior
   senator
of Massachusetts
would be the consequence of Congressional
   consent

10: The consequence would be
war

      [*10 sits down. All the others rise. Un-
      ordered movement as at the end of a con-
      ference. Then they sit down again in dif-
      ferent places.*]

LOUDSPEAKER: Washington
Secret session
of the National Security Council

PROJECTOR: George M Humphrey

Secretary of the Treasury
LOUDSPEAKER: Chairman of the Board of Directors
of the M A Hanna Company
Coal ore and steel
14: What does the projected military action
mean
in terms of our own interests
From Indochina we import
sugar tea pepper copra quinine
none of them vital commodities
and involving no investments of ours
But control of the production
of rice rubber coal and ore
would be of indirect advantage to us
since we should then deny these products
to the enemy
PROJECTOR: Charles E Wilson
Secretary of Defense
LOUDSPEAKER: President of General Motors Corporation
9: A peace treaty and the emergence of a
fractional state
under Ho Chi Minh
would lead to swift industrialisation
in a backward agricultural area
After ten years of war
the people are used to discipline
and capable of great efforts
The developments in China
which we could not halt before it was too
late
could easily repeat themselves here
PROJECTOR: John Foster Dulles
Secretary of State
LOUDSPEAKER: Partner in the firm of
Sullivan and Cromwell
Attorneys
Director of International Nickel

11: An economic boom
in a former dependent territory
would provide a significant example
to neighbouring states
It would be particularly dangerous
if a small country were permitted
to escape from Western domination
unscathed
What is this war about
[*13, 14, 15, remaining seated, form a chorus. While they are speaking softly, almost whispering, the others remain motionless. Immediately the chorus ends, the conversation is continued.*]

CHORUS: What is it about
It is to show
that revolutionary movements
must fail

PROJECTOR: Nelson A Rockefeller
Co-ordinator of Inter-American Affairs
Under Secretary of Health Education and
Welfare

LOUDSPEAKER: Co-owner of Standard Oil New Jersey
Owner of the Chase Manhattan Bank

8: The conflict in Indochina
represents an advanced stage
of what has been building up in Latin
America
for a long time
Only last year
British troops crushed a rebellion
in Guyana
In Guatemala rebels have confiscated
large areas of our plantations
thus causing
ten thousand native workers
to go over to the rebels

Terrorists threaten our oil fields
in Venezuela
From there as well as from Guatemala
the states of Central America
are being flooded
with agents spies weapons and
propaganda material
The Communist party in Brazil
has a hundred thousand members
Our good name in South America
is being undermined
mistrust and hatred
sown against us
The aim is to ruin
our export trade with the countries in this
    continent
Chile is already trying
to block our copper production and
    negotiating
an export agreement with Moscow
Forty per cent of all our private investments
are in the southern half
of the American continent

PROJECTOR: Roger Kyes
    Deputy Secretary of Defense

LOUDSPEAKER: Vice-President of General Motors
    Corporation

13: If we can no longer control
the prices of raw materials
our customary profit margins
will be untenable

PROJECTOR: Leo Welch
    Chairman of the Board of Directors
    Standard Oil Company New Jersey

7: This is the choice confronting us
Either to fight
to defend our position in the world

or to sit still and become guests
at our own funeral
Gentlemen
as the world's largest producer
trading organisation
and shareholder
the United States must
be alive to its responsibilities
political social and
economic
More than ever before
it is the government's duty
to back us
in our concerns

PROJECTOR: Harold E Talbott
Secretary of the Air Force

LOUDSPEAKER: Director of the Chrysler Corporation

15: Our armed forces can
if called on
carry out minor actions
in twenty countries at once
After the Korean war
our defense expenditure fell
but now
it is rising again
Industry can reckon with new major
contracts
before very long
I have put in for an increase
in the Air Force budget
from three and a half thousand million
to six thousand million

[*All rise. 13, 14, 15 form a chorus. They
speak quickly and softly, while the others
stand motionless.*]

CHORUS: The biggest firm in this country
is the military

with a fixed capital
of one hundred and forty thousand million
     dollars
annual expenditure in times of peace
forty thousand million dollars
It provides work
for four million workers

PHASE II

LOUDSPEAKER: Secretary of State Mr Dulles
          goes to London
          to discuss the situation
          with the British Foreign Secretary
          Anthony Eden
               [*11 as* DULLES *and 12 as* EDEN *in a formal*
               walk around the table. As they do so, the
               remainder (except 10) recite the follow-
               ing. Music begins.]
     7: In the nineteenth century
          Britain used its navy
          to keep law and order
          in the world
     8: From military bases
          Britain could maintain
          quickly and effectively
          the freedom of trade
     9: British capital
          stimulated prosperity
          in the backward areas
     13: In this century it is we
          who are ready and willing
          to assume the burden
          of leadership
     14: Averting
          through swift and flexible action

the danger
of a third world war
15: As proof of our serious intentions
we point to our newest weapon
to be successfully tested
The hydrogen bomb
[*Music ends. The speakers sit down.* DUL-
LES *and* EDEN *mount the table from direction N.*]
LOUDSPEAKER: London
Eleventh of April
Nineteen fifty-four
John Foster Dulles
with Anthony Eden
11: Before Congress can give the President
approval
for armed intervention in Indochina
the co-operation of Britain
must be assured
In that connection
I propose we now discuss conditions
for a South East Asian pact
as suggested by Churchill
12: Such a pact would indeed be extremely
helpful
in our fight against the rebels in Malaya
All the same
we must be careful
No word of it must come out
before the conference in Geneva
That could frighten off
potential allies in Asia
11: Mr Eden
Delay only increases
the danger of an invasion by China
It would be disastrous for the Western
cause

to give up Indochina without a fight
After all Mr Eden
your government too helped France
regain its foothold in Indochina
after the war

12: Mr Dulles
Military action by your country and mine
would destroy all prospects of working
    together
with the peoples of South East Asia
for years to come
Next month the rains start
making all military operations in Indochina
difficult
Even if Dien Bien Phu falls
that does not mean
the French army is finished
We must wait and see what the Viet Minh
have to propose in Geneva
Mr Dulles
Sir Winston is of the opinion
that Her Majesty's Government
is not prepared at this moment
to involve itself
in a war in Indochina

> [DULLES *and* EDEN *separate in a manner*
> *reminiscent of the end of a round in a*
> *boxing match. Both bow on opposite sides*
> *to the men seated round the table. Then*
> *they quickly approach each other again.*]

LOUDSPEAKER: Paris
Twenty-third of April
John Foster Dulles and Anthony Eden
at the French Foreign Ministry

11: Mr Eden
The French Government has just received a
    telegram

from the defenders of Dien Bien Phu
They say only a bombing attack by the
    United States
within the next three days
can save the situation
Foreign Minister Bidault confirms
that the position is desperate
We must have British support
immediately
12: Mr Dulles
We are not at the moment in a position
to take on further military commitments
Unrest in Cyprus
and a threatened rising in Aden
demand all our attention
In South East Asia our troops
are fully occupied in Malaya
11: We would carry out the necessary measures
    alone
as long as they could be presented
to the outside world
as a collective action
12: Mr Dulles
Such an act on the part of America
would lead to Chinese reprisals
and that would be the beginning
of World War Three
        [DULLES *and* EDEN *separate. They return*
        to seats at the table.]
LOUDSPEAKER: Washington
May
nineteen fifty-four
Sitting of the National Security Council
PROJECTOR: President Eisenhower
10: The stronghold of Dien Bien Phu
    surrendered early today
The conference in Geneva now

meets in the atmosphere of a French
and a Western defeat
11: No matter how many victories the enemy
gains
the people of America
will never permit
thirty million people in Viet Nam
to be subjected to a rule of force and terror
We have worked out
a counter-plan
and are about to put it into effect
Senator Mike Mansfield reports
PROJECTOR: Senator Mansfield
Expert on Indochinese affairs
8: The plan makes two clearly separate issues
The tactical aim at the Geneva conference
and the strategical aim for South East Asia
Outside the talks
we are making efforts to create
a South East Asian defense treaty
in which besides the Indonesian states
the partners will be
Britain France Australia
New Zealand the Philippines Pakistan
and Thailand
Since at Geneva
partition is the expected solution
our delegates will aim to get the dividing
line
set as far north as possible
The Viet Minh think
their victory entitles them
to claim the thirteenth parallel
way down in the south of the country
And as things stand
it would not be difficult for them
to enforce that with arms

PROJECTOR: Senator William F Knowland
                    Majority Leader
              15: Such a step can be prevented
                    only by our playing
                    on our atomic superiority
                    It is Molotov's avowed intention
                    to impress on the Chinese delegates
                    the need for circumspection
              11: We stand alone in Geneva
                    in opposing the setting up
                    of a separate Viet Minh state
                    The British are not prepared to accept
                    the military risks of our policy
                    They are concerned about the China trade
                    and the existence of Hong Kong
                    But to us no solution is acceptable
                    which entails the recognition
                    of a Communist rump state
                    To make this perfectly clear
                    I shall myself not
                    attend the conference
              15: There'll be even further difficulties
                    if the Geneva conference
                    makes neutral states of Laos
                    and Cambodia
              11: We shall not agree
                    to such a solution
                    We have made it plain in our draft
                    that these states
                    are to be regarded as protectorates
              10: My friends take care not to make
                    the dominance of the Western powers
                    too plain in the projected pact
                    or we may find ourselves accused
                    of neo-colonialism
              15: In all the countries concerned
                    the military and the police

should be made sufficiently strong
that governments can cope
with local risings
Thailand and the Philippines
as well as Burma and Japan
must receive substantial economic aid
That will reduce local unrest
and show the people the advantages
of a close tie with the Western powers

10: How do we formulate
American commitments
in the treaty

11: In the case of threats
from outside or inside any country
the member states will meet
to decide what steps shall be taken
The United States reserves the right to
    intervene
only when aggression
is of Communist origin

      [*7, 9, 13, still seated, form a chorus. They
      speak quickly and in a whispering tone,
      while the others sit motionless. Immedi-
      ately the chorus ends, the conversation
      continues as if there had been no inter-
      ruption.*]

CHORUS: So the government
of the United States
can each time say
This is a disturbance
created by
Communists
Then the government
of the United States
can put in its troops
to crush a revolt
which it says

is led
by Communists
10: How do we propose
to uphold
the neutrality of the protectorates
11: It is up to us
to see that governments are formed
which when necessary
will ask our help
in preserving their neutrality
PROJECTOR: John A Hannah
Assistant Secretary of Defense
President of Michigan State University
13: In the next few days
Emperor Bao Dai will appoint his Cabinet
in South Viet Nam
formed of trusted friends
on whom we have spent years of work
The Prime Minister
is Ngo Dinh Diem
Professor Wesley Fishel will tell you
about this distinguished man
who has much in common
with our friends Syngman Rhee
Chiang Kai-shek and Magsaysay
PROJECTOR: Wesley Fishel
Professor of Political Science
Michigan State College
7: In July nineteen fifty
I was instructed
to visit Diem in Tokio and
to invite him to the United States
for talks
Our Secret Service
had been in close contact with him
since nineteen forty-six

In the early Thirties
Diem was Minister for Home Affairs in Bao
    Dai's government
and did much then
to combat Communist terrorism
He is not only a staunch anti-Communist
but a staunch Catholic as well
During his first two years in the States
he lived as a guest
with Cardinal Spellman
In this period he made a good impression
on many people in public life
All were of the opinion
that no one was better qualified than Diem
to assume the leadership
of the free state of Viet Nam

PROJECTOR: Arthur Brandstatter
    Head of School of Police Administration
        and Public Safety
    Michigan State University

9: To prepare him for his future
    political responsibilities Diem was called
    in the year fifty-two to the Political
        Research Department
    of our university
    Together with experienced members
    of the Secret Service and experts
    in guerrilla warfare
    we drew up a detailed plan
    for the administration of South Viet Nam
    Immediately Ngo Dinh Diem is installed in
        office
    a commission of experts will journey
    to Saigon
    The first task in Saigon is to set up
    a state police department

with the following institutions
interrogation rooms internment camps
    laboratories
tracing offices and Intelligence
The card index
containing details of over six hundred
    thousand
criminal and subversive elements
will be adapted from the French
to the American system
The police will be equipped with motor
    vehicles
radios handcuffs guns and tear gas
10: How will the Secret Service participation
be camouflaged
 9: We have brought in
some professors in matters of public
    administration
from Yale Pittsburgh
and other universities
As evidence of our interest
in social reform
Professor Wolf Ladejinsky
has drafted an agricultural programme
Leo Cherne
of the International Rescue Committee
will take over the care of refugees
from the north
In the churches Cardinal Spellman
is collecting funds from the American
    people
for a new
and free Viet Nam

> [*Assistants A and B put a cardinal's robe
> around 14. 14 as* CARDINAL SPELLMAN
> *mounts the table. The others rise, then
> sit down again.*]

LOUDSPEAKER: Cardinal Francis Spellman
            addressing the American Legion
        14: In a land twelve thousand miles away
            millions of human beings are groaning
            under a dictatorial regime
            which has found new fields
            for its devilish technique
            of brainwashing
            Yet a ray of hope still remains
            In the southern part of this country
            a man has emerged
            who is prepared to fight
            for the reunification of his country
            In a part of the world
            threatened more and more
            by China's insatiable lust for power
            this man has the courage to say
            he will not be bound
            by the decisions in Geneva
            We salute this man
            who far away from us is also defending
            our country
            against brutality and godlessness
            To demonstrate our support for him
            I shall myself journey to Saigon
            and put into his hand
            the first cheque
            of our Catholic aid fund
                [CARDINAL SPELLMAN *descends from the
                table. Assistants A and B take his robe.* 7,
                8, 9, 14, 15 leave the stage.]

PHASE III

[*10 as* PRESIDENT EISENHOWER, *11 as* DULLES,
12 as EDEN *and 13 as* CHURCHILL, *standing opposite each other at the sides of the table:*

EISENHOWER N, CHURCHILL S, DULLES W,
Eden E.]
LOUDSPEAKER: Washington
Twenty-fifth of June
Nineteen fifty-four
Conference in the White House
[*All four sit down.*]
PROJECTOR: Dwight D. Eisenhower
President of the United States
PROJECTOR: Sir Winston Churchill
British Prime Minister
PROJECTOR: Anthony Eden
British Foreign Secretary
PROJECTOR: John Foster Dulles
American Secretary of State
13: The new French Prime Minister
Mendès-France
is trying to get out
on the best possible terms
He threatens to resign if
by the twentieth of July the Geneva
conference
has not found an honourable solution
He is sensible enough to see
that France's historic role
as a colonial power is nearing its end
Since it is now on the point
of giving up Indochina
our deliberations on an effective defense
policy
in the Pacific area
become of urgent moment
There can be no two opinions about that
12: In Geneva we are of course continuing
to do all we can
to strengthen France's position
Molotov is proving sympathetic

           The Soviet Union as you know
           is prepared to compromise in Asia
           in order to strengthen its hand in Europe
           Chou En-lai also
           is keen to see the fighting ended
           On the question of frontier demarcation
           we are already negotiating
           for the sixteenth parallel
      11: We cannot accept
           less than the eighteenth
      12: Molotov and Chou En-lai
           are urging the Viet Minh
           to settle for the sixteenth parallel
           We may also manage to get the seventeenth
           The Viet Minh have no other choice
           but to go along with Moscow
           They will put their hopes
           on resolving the conflict
           through free elections
      13: I have been preaching resistance
           to Communism
           since nineteen nineteen
           and I welcome the South East Asia Treaty
           which as part of the world front
           against the enemy protects
           our vital interests
           But the members must be given
           a free hand in carrying out
           their own foreign policy
           Our chief worry is
           Malaya
      12: Now the atom bomb has reduced
           the strategic importance of Suez
           we can halve the garrison there
           and thus free another forty thousand men
           for the Far East
      13: Indirectly these troops are helping

to encircle and isolate China
But China must not be provoked
into taking preventive action
against our bases
It would ease the situation
if China were admitted
to the United Nations

11: I refuse to recognise
a gang of cutthroats
as representative of the Chinese people
If the General Assembly
votes for Red China's admission
I shall propose that America
quits the United Nations

10: I too am against admitting China
to the United Nations
China already occupies North Korea
and seeks now
to take over Indochina
China is guilty of enslaving
and abducting men and women
in its own territory
China has the impertinence
to put the blame for Korea
on us
To admit China to the United
Nations would be an affront
to the principles
of our world organisation

> [*7, 8, 9, 14, 15 comes from* NW *and* NE
> *to the table. They position themselves at*
> *regular intervals around it, forming a*
> *chorus.*]

CHORUS: The Congress of the United States
signifies its rejection of the proposal
to admit the illegal Chinese government
to the Assembly of the United Nations

[7, 8, 9, 14, 15 *sit down. 11 as* DULLES, 12
as EDEN, 13 *as* GENERAL BEDELL SMITH, 14
as MENDÈS-FRANCE *mount the table.*]

LOUDSPEAKER: Paris
Thirteenth of July
Nineteen fifty-four
The French Foreign Ministry

PROJECTOR: Anthony Eden

12: Mr Dulles
If now you also
withdraw your deputy Bedell Smith
from Geneva
it will be interpreted
as a split
inside the Western alliance

PROJECTOR: John Foster Dulles

11: Mr Eden
We said last month
in Washington
the eighteenth parallel
is the least we can accept
Since Chou En-lai and
Phan Van Dong refuse
to make concessions
we can no longer take part
in the conference

PROJECTOR: General Walter Bedell Smith
U.S. Under Secretary of State

13: Our demand
for an enclave in Tonking
has also been turned down
and we have every cause to fear
that it will not be possible
to form pro-Western governments
in Laos and Cambodia

12: If you refuse at this stage
to support France

we shall not get
even the seventeenth parallel
PROJECTOR: Mendès-France
French Prime Minister
14: By withdrawing from Geneva
the United States will not
avoid a clash
Your involvement in Asia
makes a clear decision
inescapable
Chou En-lai insists
that the conference decisions
must also be signed by your government
11: We will not sign them
12: In view of your unwillingness
to approve the settlement in Geneva
I have proposed to Molotov
and Chou En-lai
that in place of signatures
the names of all participating countries
should be set down
in the preamble to the final communiqué
If the United States is not prepared
to agree even to that
then the conference has failed
and the fault
is America's
11: We suggest the following solution
[11, 12, 14 *descend from the table and
resume their seats. 13 comes forward on
the table.*]
LOUDSPEAKER: Geneva
Twenty-first of July
Nineteen fifty-four
Conclusion of the talks
Declaration of the United States
13: My government

is unable to accept
the resolutions of the conference
as they now stand
However the United States
takes note of the agreement
We shall abstain from any threat
or use of force
to its detriment
We shall regard any resumption
of hostilities
in defiance of this agreement
as a matter of grave concern
and as a serious threat
to international peace
and security
In the case of nations now partitioned
against their will
we shall continue to do all we can
to restore their unity
through free elections
We reiterate our traditional view
that all peoples have a right
to decide on their own future
The United States can subscribe
to no solution
that denies this principle

> [13 descends from the table. The others
> rise. 10, 11, 12 go off. Assistants A and B
> take away the chairs.]

PHASE IV

[6 comes from SW as hostess to PROFESSOR
FISHEL. She is wearing a close-fitting white costume in the Vietnamese style with slit sides.
7 as PROFESSOR FISHEL goes towards her. Both

    mount the table. After them 8, 9, 13, 14, 15
    separately mount the table, where they are re-
    ceived by FISHEL *and his hostess. Suggestion*
    of a cocktail party.]

LOUDSPEAKER: Saigon
    September
    Nineteen fifty-four
    Reception by Professor Wesley Fishel
        [*Assistants A and B, dressed in white,*
        come forward with drinks. There is con-
        stant movement on the table.]

PROJECTOR: Joseph Buttinger
    Historian

LOUDSPEAKER: Author of the book
    The Smaller Dragon
    A Political History of Viet Nam

    13: The Viet Minh did not really have
    to put up with the seventeenth parallel

    7: They make no fuss because they think
    the division can't last very long

    6: They imagine there will really be
    elections in two years' time

    13: Which they of course will win

PROJECTOR: Arthur Brandstatter
    Trainer of Diem's Palace Guard

    9: We're not interested in who might win
    two years from now
    Ho Chi Minh or Diem
    What we have to care about
    is much more whom we can make
    look like the probable victor
    If we can convince people
    the Viet Minh haven't a chance
    they won't vote for them

    7: Diem will never give North Viet Nam
    the chance to win an election
    because he'll take care

there'll never be an election
13: Thus proving himself
the stronger
PROJECTOR: General Edward Lansdale
C.I.A. representative
Adviser on non-conventional warfare
15: I cleared eighty thousand
Communist rebels
out of the Philippines
6: For your pal Ramon Magsaysay
15: I know
how to get the peasants
on our side
You need only to see
they get enough land
cattle and seeds
It's always the little man that matters
the rice grower the shopkeeper
the mechanic
In the Philippines I used to ride my bicycle
into the Red villages
all by myself
then sit down with the natives
tell them stories and
play my mouth organ
[*Laughter.*]
15: If you treat them right
they're as trusting as children
7: The natives in this country
have always lived in outer darkness
They've got no cultural assets
You've got to drive them to work
with a stick
They don't know the difference
between right and wrong
PROJECTOR: Naval surgeon Tom Dooley
Member of the Catholic Relief Services

LOUDSPEAKER: Author of the book
                    Deliver Us from Evil

    14: But all this misery and want in the villages
                    Men and women reduced to skeletons
                    Bodies infested with worms
                    The children with their pot bellies
                    All those hundreds of thousands of malaria
                        victims

      6: Tommy stop it
                    with your horrible stories
                    Don't spoil our evening

      9: They're all of them
                    just a shifty rabble
                    The whole crew infected
                    with the Viet Minh disease
                    How can you build up a nation
                    with people like that

    13: There are plenty of others
                    Think of our project
                    Flight from the North
                    Hundreds of thousands up there
                    fought on France's side
                    Officials landowners Catholics
                    When they see we are offering them
                    a living

      9: they'll come flocking in
                    and give us the moral victory
                    we want

PROJECTOR: Leo Cherne
                    Chairman of the Board of Directors
                    of the International Rescue Committee

LOUDSPEAKER: Co-founder of the Research Institute
                    for Management

      8: We shall pick the best
                    out of the refugees and make
                    government officials of them
                    That will give us the elite

we need
All we're lacking now
is good propaganda slogans
> [*All turn in direction NE and start to call.*]

7: Come to the south
9: Choose freedom
13: Choose a new home
14: America is sending money
15: You'll get everything you need
houses tools cattle
7: You won't have to work
You'll be well cared for
6: The Virgin Mary
has come to South Viet Nam
and calls all believers
to follow her
> [*4, 5, as refugees from North Viet Nam come slowly from NE to the table. They carry a pole with a flag. 4, 5, in black with white scarves.*]

8: There they come from the north
9: Carrying their flagpole with its dripping flag
13: The flag they've been keeping hidden
14: Their gold and red insignia
with the Pope's tiara
and Saint Peter's keys
15: Fleeing from a country
where all they hold sacred
is trodden underfoot
> [*The refugees reach the edge of the table.*]

4, 5: Whole villages are coming
led by their priests
They told us
the Virgin Mary
had gone to South Viet Nam
> [*Some leave the table, others bend down*]

> *towards the refugees. Gestures of assis-*
> *tance and good will.*]

7: Brothers and sisters from the north
8: Here you will find help
9: Tents have been prepared for you
13: We have clothes for you
14: Food and medicines
15: Only in a country
    where private enterprise has free rein
    is there so much room
    for charity
7: Where else do the great institutions
    of our great society
    act so selflessly

> [*6, 7, 8, 14 lead the refugees off towards*
> *SW with gestures of good will. 9, 13, 15*
> *follow them slowly, then remain standing*
> *in SW well to the front. Meanwhile assis-*
> *tants A and B take the table apart and re-*
> *assemble the parts again as platforms in*
> *W and E. Then 9, 13, 15 move towards*
> *S in conversation.*]

15: Refugees in their thousands
    clutter the outskirts of Saigon
13: They have no tents
    People are dying of thirst
15: Most of our economic aid
    vanishes on the black market
    The entire police force
    is involved in the racket
    Not a single officer in the army
    can be trusted
9: We shall deal with the police gangs
    by bribing the ringleaders
    Millions of dollars
    are there for the purpose
    Army officers who prove disloyal

will get no pay

13: The loafers at the roadside
    are only the poor
    the old and the sick
    The ones with brains
    or some sort of background
    have already been sorted out

 9: They will become our new middle class
    Catholics
    ten per cent of the population

15: Those we don't find jobs for
    will be given land
    What the Viet Minh gave to the peasants
    must be handed back again

13: So our agricultural experts
    will have useful places
    to raise model crops
    with the aid of the new settlers

 9: The poorer peasants will then see
    what rationalisation means
    and will learn to appreciate
    the worth of private property

        [*9, 13, 15 come close together and form a
        chorus.*]

CHORUS: Our system
    of free enterprise
    always striving
    for bigger possessions
    shall prove
    a desirable model
    for the peasants too

        [*9, 13, 15 go off in SW. The stage is
        empty for a moment.*]

PHASE V

[*1, 2, 3, 4, 5 come from NE as spokesmen for the Democratic Republic of Viet Nam. All are dressed in black. They position themselves on the raised level in N in a widely spaced row. As they speak, they come forward slowly in direction S to centre.*]

5: September
   Nineteen fifty-four
   In North Viet Nam
   most of the harvest
   has been burnt
   the dams wrecked
   the fields flooded
   Scarcely fifty miles of railway
   are still usable
   All roads badly damaged
   Half of the cattle
   destroyed
   Thousands of villages laid waste
1: Behind us
   lie fifteen years of war
   almost a century
   of colonisation
   The mines were flooded
   by the retreating French
   The quays blown up
   The fishing boats sunk
   All eleven factories
   built by France
   dismantled
   Only two power stations are still intact
   We have no capital reserves
   no food

               no machines
          2: The peasants still work
               without wheelbarrows
               scooping the water from the fields
               with buckets
               Too many still
               cannot read or write
          3: Our land reform
               starts without tractors
               without transport
               with no means of storing
               or processing
               The soil that could never
               produce enough to feed us
               must now be made
               to yield a surplus
               which we need
               to buy tools and machines
               A poor country must be turned
               into an industrial state
          4: We have only fifty engineers
               and a few hundred technicians
               Even with the experts of friendly countries
               not enough to train
               the skilled workers
               we need at once
               In this transition period
               we must rely on the ingenuity
               of all
               Where there is no iron
               tools must be made of wood
               Where there is no wood
               use bamboo sticks
          5: In building up industry
               in education
               in our health service
               in everything

this must be our constant rule
Those who know
must pass their knowledge on
to those who don't know

3: During the years of war
we took the land
that estate owners
colonists and the church
had abandoned in their flight
and gave it to the peasants
Now the peasants must be made to see
that industrial development
depends on their work
Our cadres are engaged in persuading them
that industry alone
can bring them
a better life

> [*1, 2, 3, 4, 5, turn and go off slowly in
> NE. At the same time 6, 10, 12 appear
> in SW, dressed in white. With them assis-
> tants A and B, dressed in white and carry-
> ing a mandarin's robe. At the end of the
> procession comes 11, dressed in white.
> Assistants A and B dress him in the man-
> darin's robe. Music begins.*]

10, 12: Weighed down
with the scent of roses
Ngo Dinh Diem
comes from his gardens
in his long-sleeved robe
Ngo Dinh Diem
the mandarin comes
Ngo Dinh Diem
looks into the distance
communes with his ancestors
Ngo Dinh Diem

> [*The music ends. The procession has*

reached E. 11 mounts the platform. Assis-
tants A and B behind him. 6, 10, 12 posi-
tioned irregularly at centre in front of
him.]

11: My land Viet Nam
must first of all be given
the moral foundations
on which a strong and healthy
democratic state
can be built
To consider the form
before the substance
would lead to certain failure
My duty is therefore
to root out the seeds
of corruption
Once this is done
I shall turn my thoughts
to the creation of a democracy
in the Western
sense of the word

[*8, 9, 14 from SE as American envoys,*
dressed in white. 6, 10, 12 go back to W
and stand there in a row. The American
envoys move to S, forming a row facing
N.]

8: Twenty-third of October
Nineteen fifty-four
Note from the President
of the United States of America
to Prime Minister Ngo Dinh Diem

9: We are seriously concerned
about the future
of Viet Nam

14: Artificially divided
by the Geneva agreement
weakened through long years

of war
besct by enemies
inside and out

8: The United States
is pleased to give you
Mr Diem
the help you require

9: You Mr Diem
as head of the government
must conform
to the conditions attached
to our aid

14: We expect
your government
to use this aid
to carry out the reforms
we consider
vital

8: With the money and weapons
we are sending
you Mr Diem
must enforce
loyalty to our cause

> [*8, 9, 14 take up positions in front of*
> DIEM. *13, 15, dressed in white, from* NW
> *to centre. They are dragging 3, dressed in*
> *black. They leave him lying at centre.*
> *They are followed slowly by 5, also in*
> *black.*]

13: This is the lawyer Nguyen Huu Tho
arrested
for committing acts dangerous to the state

15: He is the leader
of a conspiracy

13: Calling itself
Committee for the Defense of Peace
and the Geneva Agreement

12: It organised
the demonstration
on the first of August
in Saigon Cholon

5: It was a demonstration
to welcome
the armistice

10: It was an organised disturbance
that forced us
to fire
into the crowd
[*1 from NW, 2 from NE, 4 from SW, 7
from SE, all dressed in black, go slowly to
5 and 3 at centre. 3 rises. During this, 11
speaks as* DIEM.]

11: The chief danger
is the remnant organisation
of the Viet Minh
They are preparing
for elections
[*10, 12, 15 are given weapons by assistants
A and B.*]

13: Their troops withdrew
in accordance with the agreement
But their political cadres
stayed behind

6: They control
the whole population
in the province of Quang Nam

11: Send a regiment
to Cho Duoc
[*10, 12, 15 advance on the group of South
Viet Nam people at centre. The armed
men attempt to penetrate the group. The
group as a single body constantly evades
them.*]

4: They are tearing down our huts

2: They are cutting down the trees in our
village
1: They are building barracks
6: Break them up
when they get in your way
14: Take the names of everyone
who took part in the resistance
5: All of us
took part
3: Every child big enough
to bear loads and carry messages
was with us
8: Arrest
all the old officials
11: Offer rewards
to all who denounce
government enemies
[*1 leaps forward from the group of people.*]
1: The Geneva agreement lays down
that no one shall be persecuted
for once belonging
to the Viet Minh
6: Special compensation
should be given to all
denouncing members of their own family
11: All enemies of the new state
must be neutralised
As Prime Minister I have the right
to control the citizen's choice
of residence
to suspend the freedom of assembly
and of the press and
to give the police
unrestricted authority
1: It is now July nineteen fifty-four
the date laid down in Geneva
for the holding of elections

in both parts of Viet Nam
The Democratic Republic of Viet Nam
calls for immediate negotiations
with the representatives of South Viet Nam
> [*10, 12, 15 go to 1 and together knock him
> down. 10, 12, 15 go back to 6, 13 in W.
> The group of people closes in at once
> around 1, who gets up on his feet.*]

11: We did not sign
the Geneva agreement
We are not bound in any way
by this agreement
which was forced
on the Vietnamese people
against its will

8, 9, 14: The government of the United States
agrees with Ngo Dinh Diem
that elections cannot be held
since North Viet Nam
does not guarantee
basic democratic
rights
> [*2 comes forward from the group of South
> Viet Nam people.*]

2: The government
of the Democratic Republic of Viet Nam
proposes that the elections
should be internationally controlled
Candidates from South Viet Nam
will be allowed to campaign
> [*10, 12, 15 go to 2 and beat him up, then
> drag him away towards W, where they
> leave him lying.*]

11: Take the prisoners
to the island of Poulo Condore
> [*The group of people moves across to W
> and takes in 2, who rises.*]

2: France Great Britain
China and the Soviet Union
guarantee free elections

14: It's not Viet Minh ideas
that are dangerous
but their ability
to move the masses

11: My government protects
the right to personal initiative
It protects the right of all men
to develop
their intellectual faculties

[6, 10, 12, 13, 15 *in* W *form a chorus.*
Music begins.]

CHORUS: Only a society
that recognises
inequality
is alive
The wise
shall instruct the ignorant
Were there no
inequalities
where would one find
charity
where would one find
justice
where generosity

[*The music ends.* 6, 8, 9, 10, 12, 13, 14, 15
move quickly on the group of people, sur-
round them and herd them close together.
The group of people sinks to the ground.
6, 8, 9, 10, 12, 13, 14, 15 *go slowly back*
to their previous positions. The group of
people lies like corpses in a mass grave.
Their words are muffled and scarcely audi-
ble.]

5: We were made to dig a pit

7: We were made to stand on the edge of the
   pit
1: They bound us in twos together
2: They pushed us into the pit
4: They shovelled earth over us
6: The earth is still moving
        [8 *makes a contemptuous gesture.*]
8: Viet Cong
        [6, 8, 9, 10 *go off in SW.* 11, 12, 13, 14,
        15 *off in SE.*]

PHASE VI

[1, 2, 3, 4, 5, 7 *rise and go to the raised level
N, where they form a widely separated row,
similar to the first entry of the representatives
of North Viet Nam. They advance slowly S to
centre.*]
1: We remind people all over the world
   that according to the Geneva conference
   the demarcation line of the seventeenth
     parallel
   is only temporary
5: It was clearly stated
   that the division had no political
   or territorial significance
   Viet Nam is *one* state
2: We have repeatedly
   pressed for talks
   on elections
3: America has built a separate state
   in South Viet Nam
   A contravention
   of the Geneva agreement
   and a first step
   towards aggression

4: The powers guaranteeing this agreement
   have neither objected
   to the building of this state nor
   prepared the elections
   which should be taking place
   now
   in July nineteen fifty-six
7: We have demanded the restoration
   of rail and road services
   and postal connections
   The authorities in Saigon
   reject our demands
3: The demarcation line of the Ben Hai River
   is now the world's
   most closely sealed border
      [1, 2, 3, 4, 5, 7 turn and go off in NE.]
LOUDSPEAKER: Saigon
   June
   Nineteen fifty-seven
   Conference in the American Embassy
      [8, 9, 10, 12, 13, 15 come from SE as
      American advisers in South Viet Nam
      and as representatives of the American
      Government. Conversation begins as they
      come in and move slowly S.]
12: It would have been simpler
   if we had adopted
   the Viet Minh system of land distribution
   That would have made things better
   for the peasants
   Our land reform
   puts them back in the position of tenants
   They have to hand over a third at least
   of what they produce
9: Which gives the Viet Cong
   a good argument
15: We can meet that

effectively enough
if we do what I did
with remarkable success
· in the Philippines
Split up the families in the villages
and settle the unreliable elements
in fortified areas
which we can control
10: Why hasn't better use
been made of our money
We have sunk three thousand million
    dollars
in this country
Why can't the government
impose its authority
 8: The military budget takes care
of the training and arming
of four hundred and fifty thousand men
in the army militia and police force
Five new landing strips have been built
for heavy bombers
and several other landing strips modernised
Harbours and roads have been improved
for strategic purposes
15: Military reinforcements
have taken a large slice of our economic aid
Some also goes
on pay for officials and
military personnel
10: Why aren't conditions more stable then
 8: Our economic experts
imported cheap consumer goods
at low exchange rates
The government was supposed
to use the profits for investment
But not a cent
of all the millions earned

went into industry
let alone into land reform
It's all vanished into the pockets
of government officials
black marketeers and speculators
The market is saturated
with cheap imports
Local light industry is being choked to
    death
In Saigon alone there are
four hundred and thirteen thousand
    unemployed

13: In our main trading areas
Latin America Africa and the Middle East
the lack of local industry
is to our advantage
But here in Viet Nam
we must have private employers
or bust
Very soon we'll be hearing
how much better they do things
under the Socialist system next door

> [*Assistants A and B come from NE with
> a rolled-up red carpet. They roll it out in
> direction SW. 8, 9, 10, 12, 13, 14, 15 take
> up positions on each side of the carpet. In
> NE 11 appears as* DIEM. *A state reception
> is depicted.* DIEM *walks slowly along the
> carpet. 6 from NE follows* DIEM *as a press
> officer. As* DIEM *advances and is greeted,
> assistants A and B roll up the carpet be-
> hind him.*]

6: The President
of the Republic of Viet Nam
has arrived in New York
on a state visit

> [*10 goes to* DIEM *and embraces him.*]

6: President Eisenhower's embrace
   demonstrates the close friendship
   existing between the United States
   and the Republic of Viet Nam

10: You have accomplished
   great things
   forging a progressive
   and steadfast country
   out of chaos
      [10 *withdraws. 9 comes forward.*]

6: Robert Wagner
   Mayor of New York
   presses the hand
   of his distinguished guest

9: Rest assured
   that history
   will proclaim you
   one of the key figures
   of the twentieth century
      [9 *withdraws. 14 comes forward and em-*
      braces DIEM.]

6: Cardinal Spellman
   demonstrates with his embrace
   the close ties
   between the American episcopate
   and the patron and protector
   of the Catholic Church
   in South East Asia

14: The whole world sees in you
   the God-fearing anti-Communist
   and saviour of Viet Nam
      [14 *withdraws. 12 comes forward.*]

6: Walter S Robertson
   Assistant Secretary of State
   takes the guest's hand

12: In you
   Asia has given us a personality

whose moral strength and determination
set an example
to the whole free world
> [DIEM *and group 6, 8, 9, 10, 12, 13, 14,*
> *15 go off SW. Assistants A and B follow*
> *with the rolled-up carpet. The stage re-*
> *mains empty a few moments.*]

PHASE VII

> [*From NW come 1, 2, 3, dressed in black, and*
> *from SE 4, 5, 7, dressed in black, to centre.*
> *They represent the persecuted people of South*
> *Viet Nam. Immediately after them come 8, 9,*
> *10, 11, 12, 13, 14, 15 from SE, SW, NW and*
> *NE. They are dressed in white. Assistants A*
> *and B follow them. They form a wide ring*
> *around the people.*]

11: Saigon
Sixth of May
Nineteen fifty-nine
I proclaim
the Law Ten Fifty-nine
now in force

8: All who threaten the security
of the state will be condemned to death
by courts-martial

9: No appeal against sentence

12: For all supporting
acts of sabotage against the state
life imprisonment

11: Mayors and village inspectors
must report
all transgressions
> [*Acts of brute force are mimed. 6 comes*
> *from SW, in the same white dress as be-*

fore, to platform W. *She watches the events, unmoved.*]

6: You have only to open a window
   and at once unrest and revolution
   come flying in

13: Surround the villages

14: Search all houses

15: Seize all saboteurs
    and spies

8: Shoot them

9: Guillotine them

> [*Music begins. All in centre freeze. Several in the group of people hold one person high to represent a corpse.*]

6: Kill off a rebel or two
   to make sure they won't do it again
   and what do the people do
   Bring in the corpse and complain

> [*Music ends. The mimed display continues.*]

12: There they come

13: All over the place

14: Ex-Viet Minh

15: Forcing the villagers
    into acts of violence
    against our officials

> [*Music begins. All freeze again.*]

6: They've got Communism like a disease
   slaughtering all who come near
   committing all sorts of atrocities
   Make them see who's master here

> [*Music ends. Resumption of mimed display.*]

8: Drive them out of their houses

9: Drive them out of the villages

10: Burn down their houses

12: Destroy the rice stocks

11: Break up the village communities
    Split up the families
13: Put them in camps
        [*Music begins. All freeze once more.*]
 6: Hundreds of thousands are being shifted
    concentrated grouped and sifted
    Once safely under lock and key
    they'll be out of reach of the enemy
        [*End of music. The representatives of the
        Diem government and the American ad-
        visers move away from the group of Viet
        Nam people. These all stand close to-
        gether, their hands and arms behind their
        backs, as if bound. 6, 8, 9, 10, 11, 12, 13
        go off in SW and SE. 14, 15, remain in
        front of the group.*]
14: You will build
    your strategic hamlet
    as instructed
    by American experts
15: First you dig
    a moat
14: After that double palisades
    and wire netting
15: Control towers for the sentries
14: Now living quarters for the garrison
15: Then barrack huts
14: Thirty people to each hut
15: One government supervisor
    to each group
14: The barracks
    will be numbered
15: Each villager
    will have a number
14: Villagers will march to work
    in groups

15: No going out
after work

14: Nobody to leave the camp
without a pass

15: All who infringe village regulations
will be beaten

14: Or for grave offenses
executed

> [*14, 15 drive the group in front of them
> in direction SE. All go off. The stage is
> empty. 1, 2, 3, as representatives of the
> Democratic Republic of Viet Nam, come
> in NE and move to N. All are dressed in
> black.*]

1: Twenty thousand people
murdered in the south
A hundred and fifty thousand
held in prisons
and concentration camps
Nine million
are to be cooped up
in fortified villages

2: The United States is legally pledged
to respect the Geneva agreement
Its perpetual infringement of the agreement
together with the government in Saigon
gives us the right
to take counter-measures

1: We must come to the help
of the rebel movement in the south
Viet Nam is a single state
We can move freely within this state
without being accused
of aggression

3: Our policy is what it has always been
To insist on the fulfillment

of the Geneva agreement
We have countered our opponents'
    infringements
only with diplomatic protests
We have avoided the use of force
in support of our rights
We have worked to rebuild
our part of the country
economically and culturally
We have attempted
to apply the principles of peaceful
    co-existence
to our own situation
4: Co-existence is possible
only when a Socialist state
is strong enough
to stand up to
the imperialist aggressor
Of all Socialist states only the Soviet Union
can do that
We are not yet strong enough
to take on the United States
3: We are engaged in a sociological
competition with the south
The principle we follow is
that in a new Socialist state
economic and cultural progress
must take precedence over all else
On what is achieved in our republic
depends the freedom
of all Viet Nam
All we can do
to consolidate the north
also helps to strengthen
the revolutionary movement
in the occupied territories
4: We know the enemy

is doing all he can
to stamp out resistance
We know too that the more we achieve
and the more the regime in Saigon
fails to achieve
the greater the threat of aggression
against us
1: Every day we hear new slogans
aimed at the liberation
of the north
Every day we arrest
spies sent to commit
acts of sabotage in our territory
3: We must not let ourselves be provoked
by Diem
or by the United States
We have at this moment no choice
but to let the south fight on alone
while we use the time
still remaining
to prepare ourselves
for the direct attack
the Americans are planning
      [*1, 2, 3, 4, go off in NE.*]

PHASE VIII

[*9, 12, 13, 14, 15 as American advisers come in
from SE. Conversation begins as they enter.*]
LOUDSPEAKER: Saigon
December
Nineteen sixty
Planning conference
of American advisers
13: The people's resistance
has grown to such proportions

that the fall of Diem's government
is now only a matter of time
His soldiers cannot be trusted
Thousands go over to the Viet Cong
every month
Only our own troops now
can save the situation

14: For that we need
Congress' approval
And we'll get that only
if the Communists attack

12: If we increase the number of advisers
and bring in troops gradually
we'll force Ho Chi Minh
to give up his policy
of non-intervention

15: We won't be able to use our own forces in
strength
until we have convinced Congress
that North Viet Nam is smuggling
men and arms into the south

13: The aggressive intentions of the north
must be presented
as a fact

9: On the workings of the anti-Communist
mind
this cannot fail
to make its effect
For what are we trying to do
          [*12, 14, 15 close up and form a chor-
          us. They speak softly, almost whispering,
          while the others remain motionless. When
          the chorus ends, the conversation is im-
          mediately resumed.*]

CHORUS: For what are we trying to do
We are trying
to strike at the root

of revolution
13: Since nineteen fifty-four
the Democratic Republic of Viet Nam
has been altogether too successful
Agricultural and
industrial production
has risen far above
the pre-war figures
Skilled workers and technicians
have been trained
in next to no time at all
At the end of the war there wasn't a single
    machine
in working order
Now machines
and tools are being exported
Almost all villages have their schools
kindergartens and medical centres
In nineteen thirty-nine there were
sixty doctors
Now they have over two thousand
Mass diseases such as tuberculosis
smallpox cholera typhus and malaria
have all been wiped out
by improved hygiene
Their victory over hunger
illness and poverty
must in justice be regarded
as a historic achievement
What we must do is
destroy the people's trust
in their revolutionary leaders

> [1, 2, 3, *from SW and* 4, 5, 6, *from SE as*
> *members of the National Liberation Front*
> *in South Viet Nam. All dressed in black.*
> 1, 2, 3 *first in direction NW,* 4, 5, 6 *in*
> *direction NE. They then turn towards*

centre and close in to a row. They move
in direction S, driving 9, 12, 13 off in SW,
14, 15 off in SE.]

5: The people of South Viet Nam
make the following demands

3: The dictator's regime must be smashed

4: The occupying power thrown out

1: A National Assembly elected

2: Political prisoners freed

3: Concentration camps closed

2: Fortified villages destroyed

1: Rents must be reduced

5: Land fairly divided

6: People taught to read and write

1, 2, 3, 4, 5: These are our demands

3: They are heard everywhere
in the streets squares and market places

6: Many have been imprisoned
or have died for them

2: For these demands
we will bring out
our weapons again
[*1, 2, 3, 4, 5, 6 form a chorus.*]

CHORUS: Twentieth of December
Nineteen sixty
The National Front
for the Liberation of South Viet Nam
is founded
to fight
with words and arms
for a national rising
[*1, 2, 3 off in SW, 4, 5, 6 off in SE. The*
stage is empty.]

PHASE IX

*[8, 9, 10, 11, 12, 14, 15 come from NW, NE,
SW, and SE. All are dressed in white. They
take up positions suggestive of a very concentrated discussion.]*

LOUDSPEAKER: Washington
October
Nineteen sixty-one
Secret session in the White House
John F Kennedy
President of the United States

10: Gentlemen
The battlefield for the defense of freedom
lies today in the southern hemisphere
In Asia Latin America and Africa
where the peoples' hopes
are greatest
The enemies of freedom
want to destroy these hopes
This is a struggle of wills
as well as of arms
It is a fight to win hearts
as well as a fight for existence
General Maxwell Taylor
who has just come from Saigon
will tell you of our plans
for a special war in Viet Nam

LOUDSPEAKER: General Maxwell D Taylor
The President's Military Representative

12: The Communist leaders are trying
to undermine
the position of the United States in Asia
They mean to demonstrate that
wars of liberation as they call them

are a sure and successful way
of spreading militant Communism
We will show them
that wars of liberation are not
sure and successful but
unsure and doomed to failure
We will destroy
the myth of their infallibility
in order to shield
all the other threatened nations
from further subversion

10: I have consequently given orders
for the working out of a new
anti-guerrilla strategy
Our atomic superiority
is of no use to us here
Our forces must be taught
new techniques

LOUDSPEAKER: Major General Edward Lansdale

15: Guerrillas can be defeated
only with the help
of the people
My view has always been
that we must give the people of South Viet
  Nam
something to fight for
In principle I was in favour
of strategic hamlets
But so much compulsion was needed
to get them built
that inevitably
we lost the people's confidence

10: General Lansdale
You do not tell us
how we can now win back
the people's confidence

15: Mr President
According to our information
that is impossible
under present conditions
All our considerable aid
has not succeeded
in producing a stable government
The ruling classes are not prepared
to work for social improvements
More than three-quarters
of the South Vietnamese people
side with the Liberation Front

10: In my opinion
the most urgent social reform
is to separate the people
from the guerrillas
Professor Eugene Staley
and General Maxwell Taylor
have drawn up a plan to effect this

LOUDSPEAKER: Eugene Staley
Professor of International Economy
at Stanford Research Institute
The President's Political Representative

9: We must start by acknowledging
that the Communists have already succeeded
in creating the conditions for success
in the south
It would be wrong to say they have achieved
    this
through terrorism
All they have done
is to apply Mao Tse-tung's recipe
for making a sea
on which they can move unhindered
Our task
is to dry up that sea

12: This is the plan
aimed at pacifying South Viet Nam
within eighteen months
Phase one
Consolidation of Diem's government
Strengthening of our bases
Complete control over the people
concentrated in sixteen thousand fortified
    villages
9: Phase two
To build up the pacified south
economically socially
and politically
12: Phase three
To build up Diem's army
civil guard police and militia
half a million men in all
To increase the number of our experts
to fifteen thousand
To bring in planes
artillery and tanks
followed by a gradual build-up
of men and material
9: Phase four
Start of air attacks
on military targets in North Viet Nam
thus showing the people in the south
that we are in a position
to inflict punishment
on the northern government
they so much admire
10: Once we join in the fighting
we must carry it on
to victory
To give way
to a little country of Asian peasants

a hundred times smaller than our own
would be to encourage revolution
in other parts of the world
15: The British
needed thirteen years
and two hundred and sixty thousand men
to quell eight thousand guerrillas
in Malaya
Reckoning from that proportion
of one to thirty
we should need half a million men
for the fifteen thousand
partisans in South Viet Nam
And the figure won't stay
at fifteen thousand
12: Our strategy is different
from that of the British
We shall not just fight the guerrillas
hand to hand
Our method is this
On the one hand
swift surprise attacks
Guerrilla tactics
with the most modern equipment
Troop landings
from helicopters
Wide reconnaissance
with electronic gear
Amphibian vehicles for crossing swamps
and flooded fields
And on the other hand
systematic bombing
of selected areas
which we declare to be free zones
That is to say
no definite targets but

total destruction of all growth
by napalm and toxic chemicals
This takes away the peasants' food supply
for years ahead
and forces them
to seek protection
in government areas
LOUDSPEAKER: Senator Mike Mansfield
8: How can operations on this scale
be put over to the public
10: Senator Mansfield
we are working at the moment
on a White Paper
The Secretary of State will explain
our line of argument
PROJECTOR: Dean Rusk
Secretary of State
11: The White Paper is based on the argument
that aggression stems from the north
The rebels are not
in our view
the true enemy
So we are not intervening
in an internal conflict
in South Viet Nam but
preventing aggression from outside
We maintain that since Geneva
the economic situation in the north
has been growing steadily worse
South Viet Nam on the other hand
has made great strides
And it is to destroy what has been done
    there
that the Communists are infiltrating into
    the south
South Viet Nam is too weak

to resist the aggressor alone
As allies it is our duty
to come to their aid
8: Reports from our Secret Service
show quite clearly
that there has been no planned infiltration
from the north
The few captured partisans
who came from North Viet Nam
had been living in the south
before nineteen fifty-four
They were simply returning
to their families
And it is known from seized weapons
that the guerrillas are getting more than
eighty per cent of their equipment
from South Vietnamese stocks
12: Mr Mansfield
we are simply covering ourselves
Before long we shall have formulated
proof of an aggression
11: Our main concern is to increase
our striking power
and in such a way that everything we do
looks like a reaction
to enemy provocation
By the time the world gets wise to it
it will have been done
In any case gentlemen
you all know it is not Viet Nam
but China we are really concerned with
Within five years China
with its seven hundred million people
will have the atom bomb
The Yellow Peril
is not just a phrase

10: If our plans for South Viet Nam do not
achieve the desired result
we put Phase Four into operation
in the way worked out
by Professor Rostow

LOUDSPEAKER: Walt Whitman Rostow
Department of State

14: The build-up of our bases
will lead to increased
guerrilla activity
This justifies a further strengthening
of our defenses
Every Viet Cong attack
gives us an excuse
for counter-measures
If one of our depots
is destroyed
then we bomb
the enemy supply lines
With each terrorist act
we take a further step forward
For example
we get South Vietnamese torpedo-boats
to shell North Vietnamese
coastal stations
This forces the North Vietnamese ships
out to sea
Our naval forces
will be on regular patrol duty
in the Gulf of Tonking
disregarding
the twelve-mile limit
Should our vessels be attacked
we report provocation
in international waters
and sink the enemy's ships

Aircraft carriers standing by
move in to effect reprisals
on the mainland
12: First we bomb
military and industrial installations
Then we go on to destroy
cultivated areas
power stations and
road networks
8: And if this doesn't stop them
12: Then we attack
villages and towns
Important targets
in the social infrastructure are
schools housing blocks
churches pagodas
and hospitals
8: And if even this doesn't break
the people's resistance
12: We destroy the locks dykes and dams
10: For us Viet Nam
is a test case
How to crush an enemy
anywhere
who is militarily weak
but politically
our superior
In South East Asia
we are not yet fighting for our lives
But we are learning there
how to fight for our lives
when that day
really comes

> [*All move quickly apart. 11 to SW, 10 to
> NE. 11 is again dressed by assistants A
> and B in* Diem's *white mandarin's robe.*

> *11 as* DIEM *and 10 as* KENNEDY *each re-*
> *ceive a megaphone from the assistants.*
> DIEM *and* KENNEDY *stand opposite each*
> *other in corners SW and NE.*]

LOUDSPEAKER: Fourteenth December
Nineteen sixty-one
President Ngo Dinh Diem
to the President of the United States
John F Kennedy
> [11 *calls through the megaphone.*]

11: The Republic of Viet Nam
like your country
has fought constantly
in the service of peace
We have honoured
the Geneva agreement
We have called repeatedly
for free elections
The north has never ceased
its efforts to force
its Communist regime
on our people
Growing streams
of Communist agents
weapons and soldiers
pour into our land
Officials village inspectors
loyal citizens
are murdered daily
Mr President
My people and I
know how much
we already owe
to the United States
Now however only
total mobilisation

can bring us victory
over the Viet Cong
Mr President
America's friendship
America's money
weapons and troops
will help us
to achieve our aim
[10 *calls through his megaphone.*]
10: Deeply alarmed
and shocked
by the onslaught
on your country
we are sending
at once
everything you need
to defend
free Viet Nam
[11 *takes off the mandarin's robe. Assistants A and B go off with robe and megaphones.*]

PHASE X

[8, 9, 10, 11, 12, 13, 14, 15, *all dressed in white, form two choruses.* CHORUS I, *consisting of* 8, 9, 10, 11, *at centre* W. CHORUS II, *consisting of* 12, 13, 14, 15, *at centre* E. *All turned to* S *in static poses.*]
CHORUS I: Just by being there
North Viet Nam endangers
the social order
we are trying to establish
in the Republic of Viet Nam
CHORUS II: How could you ever

tolerate a shift
in the balance of power
How could you ever
allow your world markets
to shrink

CHORUS I: Three thousand three hundred
military bases
protect our interests
at strategic points
throughout the world

CHORUS II: Your huge corporations
control sixty per cent
of the world's
raw materials

CHORUS I: Our system of world dominance
creates jobs
for millions

CHORUS II: Through armaments and war
you cover up
the permanent crisis
within your system

CHORUS I: Our system produces
surplus
to a degree never known before

CHORUS II: One man in three is poor
under your system
They live
herded together
in crumbling houses
Ignorance
holds them down
Anger is rising
in the big cities
Your slum dwellers
march in thousands
through the streets
demanding the rights

which the men in power
refuse them

CHORUS I: We have a vision
of the Great Society
assuring
sanctity of life
increased knowledge
higher living standards
to all
But around us
in jungles and deserts
sit countless millions
who begrudge us
our wealth
So now
we have no choice
but to use our surplus
to defend
our system

CHORUS II: Yes
we see
what you are doing
with your surplus
Making war planes
rockets bombs
tanks automobiles
and television sets
on which you show us
day and night
generals and film stars
burning villages
piles of corpses
ruins and twisted metal
Yes
we see
what you are doing
with your surplus

CHORUS I: We the planners
who know all that's going on
can now prove
that our fleet
has been deliberately attacked
in the Gulf of Tonking
We sank the two ships
that threatened us
and then destroyed
the remains of the fleet
in harbour
We sent in planes
from our aircraft carriers
to effect reprisals
on oil and supply depots

LOUDSPEAKER: Washington
Fifth of August
Nineteen sixty-four
President Lyndon B Johnson
before Congress
[10 *takes a step forward from* CHORUS I.]

10: I Lyndon B Johnson
continuing the policies laid down
by previous Presidents
for the Far East
intend to make sure
that all attacks
on the free nations of Asia
are effectively repulsed
I now demand from Congress
full authority
to act in the way I consider
urgent and necessary
[10 *steps back into* CHORUS I. 1, 2, 4, *from*
NW, 3, 5, 6, 7 *from NE, all dressed in*
black, form a row on the raised level N as
CHORUS III.]

CHORUS III: The paddy field is a pregnant woman
The sprouting rice wilts in terror
The fields are roaring and erupting
We call the dead loudly by name
The sprouting rice chars in the fire
Sow new seed in the fields
Do not be frightened as you gather the rice
Sling the loaded gun over your back
Cut the rice quickly before they come
Take care the sun does not blind you
when you raise your gun

CHORUSES
I AND II: Both houses of Congress
assent to the President's request
and give him full authority
to act in the way
he considers urgent and necessary
for the defense of freedom

PHASE XI

[CHORUS I *moves back to form a row facing*
E. CHORUS II *moves back to form a row facing*
W. 1, 2, 3, 4, 5, 6, 7 *walk singly towards S be-*
tween CHORUSES I *and* II. *There they form a*
widely spaced line, leaving room for 3 in the
middle.]

1: Be prepared
for the worst
You in the fields
get used
to sowing and reaping
in smoke and poison
You on the dykes
have earth
and stones ready

      to fill the craters

6: Be prepared
    for the worst
    You in the villages
    dig pits to hide in
    Make shelters too
    for your goats and buffaloes
    You in the schools
    get used
    to teaching and learning
    while bombs are falling

7: Be prepared
    for the worst
    You in the cities
    keep on working
    Put out the fires
    then back to your jobs
    You in the factories
    with your steady hands
    move swiftly between
    the machines and the guns

4: Be prepared
    for the worst
    You in the streets
    put sand heaps
    everywhere
    for filling the cracks
    You on the bridges
    build strong rafts
    and after the attack
    string them together

2: Be prepared
    for the worst
    You doctors and nurses
    get used
    to treating wounds

by candlelight
Hide your patients
in the jungle
Work untiringly
to save lives
5: Be prepared
for the worst
The enemy will try
to destroy
all we have built
in this land
The enemy will try
to kill
all living things
in our land

[*3 comes slowly forward. Very quietly.*]

3: This mighty enemy
follows in the footsteps
of all our previous
oppressors
You see
how hard he tries
to thwart the power
of revolution

[*1, 2, 3, 4, 5, 6, 7 as* CHORUS III]

CHORUS III: The storms
he unleashes
we can survive
We will outlive
him too
Time is on our side
We do not stand
alone

[*Dissolution of* CHORUSES I, II *and* III.
All move slightly forward towards S, *where
they form a long unordered line. All take*

part in the final chorus.]

FINAL
CHORUS: But the aggressor
is divided
The front line runs
through his own land
The voice of protest
against the havoc
he is causing
grows louder
The humbled
and distressed
have had enough
of their submission
Every day
shots ring out
in the ghettoes
of their cities
And now they see
the weak
will not yield
to their force
they offer peace
Many are glad
But what do they mean
by peace
Will peace
remove the cause
for which
they attacked us
Will peace
bring freedom
to all who rose
to win it
We know
as long as they rule
with all the great power

of their wealth
nothing will change
What we have shown
is the beginning
The fight goes on

CHRONOLOGY

PART ONE

PHASE I

c. 500 BC   Chinese mariners trade with the empire of Funan, in the south of present-day Viet Nam.

c. 400 BC   The kingdom Van Lang, existing according to legend since 2879 BC in the region between the lower Yangtze and the Red rivers: predecessor of the Viet empire.

333 BC   Chinese expansion drives the Viet people towards the south; era of the Hundred Principalities (Boach Viet) in the area of present-day Kwangsi, Kwangtung, Tonking and Annam.

258 BC   Founding of the kingdom of Au Lac (Viet Lac).

255–206 BC   The emperor Shih Huang Ti of the Tsin dynasty unites the Chinese empire; further expansion to south; building of the Great Wall in the north.

c. 200–196 BC   The Chinese general Trieu Da conquers the kingdom of Au Lac; he adopts Vietnamese customs and extends the country in the north and south; proclaims himself emperor of independent Nam Viet in 196 BC.

196 BC   First written records of a Viet state, recognised by the emperor Liu Fang of the Han dynasty as an independent state under China and named Nam Viet by the Chinese.

111 BC Nam Viet annexed by the Chinese Han dynasty.

111 BC–30 AD Some Chinese nationals settle in Nam Viet owing to economic difficulties in China; direct Chinese administration introduced.

40 AD Revolt by Vietnamese feudal nobility against Chinese rule, led by the sisters Trung Nhi and Trung Trac.

c. 200–600 Development of the empire of Funan across the southern part of present-day Cambodia and Viet Nam; cultivation of the Mekong delta; building of the complicated irrigation system; decentralised and feudal system of administration.

PHASE II

627 Fall of the Funan empire.

679 Nam Viet becomes a Chinese protectorate under the Tang dynasty and is named An Nam by the Chinese.

907 The empire of Champa comprises the present-day Vietnamese provinces of Quang Nam, Binh Dinh, Nha Trang and Phan Trang.

939 Rule of the Ngo dynasty in Nam Viet, now formally independent of China.

968 Dinh Bo Linh ascends the throne. The country is named Da Co Viet, or Viet Nam. Since this time contemporary Vietnamese historians refer exclusively to Viet Nam.

PHASE III

980 Dinh De Toan, emperor of An Nam, in campaign against Champa.

981 Beginning of the early Le dynasty.

1009–1225 Late Li dynasty. Introduction of a centralised administration and expansion of the empire in the south (Champa); system of buying and selling official posts introduced; general conscription; construction of a comprehensive road network with mail stations.

1044 The Cham armies totally destroyed by the emperor of Viet Nam, Phat Ma.

1244 The dykes in the Red River delta constructed up to the coast under the emperor Tran Thai Tong of the Tran dynasty.

1258 Marco Polo visits Champa and parts of present-day Cambodia; discovers the holy city of Angkor.

1284 Mongolian invasion of Viet Nam under Kublai Khan; the Vietnamese army raised to 500,000 men and the attack repelled.

1312 Champa becomes a province of Viet Nam.

1400 Hy dynasty in Viet Nam.

1406 Chinese armies under the Ming emperor Cheng Tsu attack Viet Nam.

PHASE IV

1406–1427 Under the leadership of Le Loi a prolonged guerrilla war is waged against the occupying powers; after the liberation, administration reorganised and land reforms introduced; Le Loi proclaims himself first emperor of the late Le dynasty.

1460–1470 Emperor Le Thanh Tong; expansion in south with peasant armies; publication of a legal code with emphasis on women's rights.

1471 Fall of the Champa empire. Viet Nam attains its present boundaries.

1527 Emperor Mac Dang Dung of Viet Nam puts

himself under Chinese domination in order
to fight against the Le dynasty.

1532   For the emperor Le Trung Ton, Nguyen Kim
and Trinh Kiem reorganise the army to fight
against the Mac dynasty; Trinh take over
power in the north of Viet Nam (Le dynasty) and Nguyen in the south.

c. 1500   First landing of Portuguese and Dutch sea-
farers in Viet Nam; establishment of mis-
sionary and trading stations.

1500–1600   Struggle for power among the Mac, Trinh
and Nguyen.

1615   The Portuguese Joao de Cruz builds a gun
factory near Hue to aid the Nguyen in the
south.

1627   The Mac dynasty finally defeated by the
Trinh; Alexander de Rhodes establishes a
French mission in Tonking.

1637   A Dutch trading station opened in Hien
Nam (Tonking).

1643   The Nguyen fleet defeats a Dutch squadron
supporting the Trinh.

1680   The first French trading station opened in
the Red River delta.

1698   The Nguyen take Saigon with Portuguese
armed assistance.

1763   France loses its Indian possessions and turns
its colonial ambitions towards Indochina.

1771   Beginning of the Tay Son resistance, both to
the Trinh and the Nguyen.

1776   The Tay Son take Saigon; Nguyen Nhac, one
of the three Tay Son brothers, proclaims himself emperor.

PHASE V

1777   Nguyen Anh, the last of the Nguyen line, takes Saigon with French help.

1778   Nguyen appoint Nguyen Anh heir to the dynasty; after a long struggle he defeats the Tay Son army.

PHASE VI

1801   Nguyen Anh takes the cities of Hue and Hanoi with French assistance and proclaims himself emperor under the name Gia Long.

1820–1841   Under the rule of the emperor Ming Mang, the resistance of the Vietnamese upper classes against the French colonisers begins.

1841–1847   The persecution of Christians in the reign of emperor Thieu Tri gives the French grounds for intervention.

1843   The corvette *Héroine* "rescues" five missionaries in Hue; the European colonial powers and the USA win for themselves more and more extra-territorial rights.

1847   The cruisers *Gloire* and *Victorieuse* threaten Da Nang.

1858   Da Nang (Tourane) attacked and occupied by the French.

1859   Saigon taken by the French.

1858–1860   Anglo-French attack on China (Opium War); French warships land on the Vietnamese coast.

1862–1867   Cochin-China occupied by troops of Napoleon III.

PHASE VII

1873   Hanoi taken by the French.

1883–1884   Treaties of Hue, in which the French establish a protectorate over Tonking and Annam.

1884–1886   The French take Cambodia.

1886–1896   Rebellion of the Vietnamese intelligentsia against French rule.

1896   The French take Laos.

1905   Japanese victory over Russia; Asian nationalism grows in strength.

PHASE VIII

1919   Nguyen Ai Quoc (Ho Chi Minh) presents the Versailles peace conference with a manifesto demanding self-determination for Viet Nam.

1920   Nguyen Ai Quoc (Ho Chi Minh) takes part in the congress at Tours to establish the French Communist party; in June of this year Lenin publishes his essays on national and colonial questions.

1925   Founding of the revolutionary League of Vietnamese Youth (Thanh Nien).

1926   Bao Dai ascends the throne.

1926–1927   Chiang Kai-shek's liquidation campaign against the Communists in China.

1930   Amalgamation on 3 February of the three Communist parties and establishment of the Communist party of Viet Nam (Dong Duong Cong Sa Dong) by Nguyen Ai Quoc (Ho Chi Minh).

PHASE IX

1930–1931 Resistance movements in the provinces Nghe An and Binh Dinh, in Phu Rien, Dao Tieng, Xa Cat, Sa Dec, Vinh Long, Tuon Thi, Hue, Saigon and Hai Phong; establishment of revolutionary committees of workers and peasants; the French colonial power imposes sanctions, shells rebellious villages and towns, 30,000 Vietnamese murdered; massive entries to Communist trade unions and peasants' organisations.

1932 Communist underground movement set up in Viet Nam; start of Japanese aggression against China.

PHASE X

1936 Front Populaire government in France legalises the political struggle in Viet Nam; Vo Nguyen Giap and Pham Van Dong found the Indochinese Democratic Front; establishment of the Indochinese Congress and setting up of more than 600 action committees by the Communist party.

1939 Start of Japanese aggression against Indochina; the Communist party goes underground again; Communist party takes over the leadership of the anti-imperialist struggle in Viet Nam.

1940 The Viet Nam Communist party prepares the people for a general uprising.

1941 The Viet Minh founded in June (Viet Nam Doc Lap Dong Minh Hoi).

1944   On 20 January President Roosevelt assures
       the British ambassador, Lord Halifax, that
       France will not be permitted to return to In-
       dochina, and that Viet Nam will be placed
       under an international mandate.

       On 22 December Vo Nguyen Giap founds
       the Vietnamese Liberation Army.

PHASE XI

1945   On 9 March armed resistance begins on a
       wide front against the Japanese occupiers.

       On 13 August a provisional government takes
       over in Hanoi; the August revolution ends in
       victory.

       On 2 September the Democratic Republic of
       Viet Nam is established; President Ho Chi
       Minh proclaims Vietnamese independence
       in Hanoi.

       On 13 September British troops under Gen-
       eral Gracey land in Saigon with instructions
       to disarm Japanese troops south of the six-
       teenth parallel on behalf of the Allies.

       On 14 September National Chinese troops
       land in North Viet Nam with instructions to
       disarm Japanese troops north of the sixteenth
       parallel on behalf of the Allies.

       On 23 September General Gracey, urged by
       the French government, proclaims a state of
       emergency in Saigon; 5,000 Japanese soldiers,
       armed by the British, start fighting against
       the Viet Minh administration.

1946   On 1 January French troops begin to "clean
       up" in South Viet Nam; the British troops
       withdraw; free elections in the whole of Viet
       Nam; of 400 seats in the National Assembly

the Viet Minh win 330, the non-Socialist nationalists 70.

On 6 March a temporary agreement is reached between France and the Democratic Republic of Viet Nam; France recognises Viet Nam as a free state within the Indochinese Federation and the French Union.

On 31 May the National Chinese troops withdraw from North Viet Nam.

On 14 September a *modus vivendi* reached between the Democratic Republic of Viet Nam and France; currency and customs union in Indochina pending new negotiations; the agreement of 6 March confirmed; further talks arranged for March 1947.

On 9 November the National Assembly of Viet Nam approves a constitution.

On 23 November the French bomb the Vietnamese residential area of Hai Phong: more than 6,000 residents killed.

On 19 December general state of war between the Democratic Republic of Viet Nam and France; start of the so-called Indochinese war.

1947 In August talks in Hong Kong between the U.S. representative, William Bullitt, and Bao Dai.

On 22 September William Bullitt meets the French High Commissioner in Indochina, Emile Bollaert.

1949 On 8 March France recognises Bao Dai's government as the legal government of an "independent Viet Nam within the French Union."

On 18 July the United States welcomes the establishment of Bao Dai's government as providing the basis "for a progressive realisation of the Vietnamese people's just demands"; start of American support for the French colonial war with the object of forcing France out of Indochina.

In December the commander of the U.S. Air Force in the Far East, Stratemeyer, and the head of the C.I.A. in Japan, Willoughby, arrive in Viet Nam.

1950 On 2 February the United States officially recognises Bao Dai's government.

On 6 March an American economic delegation under Robert Allen Griffin arrives in Saigon; enquiry into the possibilities of American investment in Indochina and American economic aid for Bao Dai's government.

On 16 March the aircraft carrier *Boxer* and the cruisers *Stickell* and *Anderson* enter Saigon harbour.

On 2 June Dean Acheson declares American determination to support the French in the war in Indochina.

On 27 June President Truman officially announces a speed-up in the provision of military support for France and its allies in Indochina and the despatch of a military mission.

On 10 August the first American war supplies arrive in Saigon.

1952 On 12 October the 200th aid consignment from the United States arrives in Saigon.

1953 In June the Navarre Plan for the "pacification" of Indochina within eighteen months is put into effect.

On 31 July the U.S. Congress resolves to grant France a sum of 400 million dollars for the war in Indochina.

On 20 November the first air landing of French troops is made in Dien Bien Phu.

PART TWO

PHASE I

1954   On 27 January the American Embassy in
Saigon reveals the amount of aid supplied
by the United States to France: 400,000 tons
of war material, 1,400 tanks, 340 airplanes,
350 warships, 15,000 radio sets, 150,000 light
weapons, 255 million rounds of ammunition
of all calibres.

On 6 February the American Department of
Defense places B-26 bombers and 200 air
mechanics at France's disposal.

On 13 March United States aid in the Indochinese war has reached a total of over 2
billion dollars; according to Christian Pineau,
member of the Finance Commission of the
French National Assembly, the United States
bears 78.25 per cent of the costs to France's
21.75 per cent.

On 22 March the Supreme Commander of
the French army goes to Washington to request American aid in the relief of Dien Bien
Phu; "Operation Vautour" provides for the
use of 60 heavy B-29 bombers and 300 fighters
over Dien Bien Phu; the use of atom bombs
is discussed.

On 4 April President Eisenhower refers to a
previous proposal by Churchill and suggests
to the British Prime Minister an alliance between the United States, Britain, France,
Thailand, the Philippines, Australia and New
Zealand directed against the liberation movements in South East Asia.

PHASES II AND III

1954   Between 26 April and 21 July talks in Geneva
on the ending of hostilities between France
and the Viet Minh.
On 7 May the stronghold of Dien Bien Phu
capitulates.
On 18 June the United States brings Ngo
Dinh Diem to Saigon.

PHASE IV

On 7 July Ngo Dinh Diem is installed as
Prime Minister in Saigon.
On 2 August Diem's troops open fire at a
celebration in Kim Doi welcoming the Geneva agreement: 17 killed, 67 wounded.
On 16 August Diem's troops open fire at a
celebration in the province of Go Cong welcoming the Geneva agreement: 8 killed, 200
wounded; three people killed in Piem Ai for
the same reason—i.e., welcoming the Geneva agreement.

PHASE V

1954   On 4 September Diem's troops attack the
villages Ha Lam and Cho Duoc in the Quang
Nam province and kill 39 inhabitants; 55
villagers taken prisoner and tortured, 37 more
wounded.
On 7, 8, and 9 September Diem's troops kill
80 inhabitants in attacks on the villages Ngan
Son and Chi Thanh in the province of Phu
Yen; 46 others wounded, and hundreds taken
prisoner and tortured.

On 8 September SEATO is founded, illegally declaring south Viet Nam, Laos and Cambodia protectorates.

Between 13 and 18 September Diem's troops kill 500 inhabitants of villages in Mo Cay, Ben Tre Province; 300 taken prisoner and tortured.

On 23 October President Eisenhower promises, in a letter, American support for Ngo Dinh Diem in rebuilding the Republic of Viet Nam.

On 7 November the Diem government arrests the members of the Saigon-Cholon Peace Committee, among them the lawyer Nguyen Huu Tho, who later becomes President of the National Liberation Front.

On 25 December the International Control Commission for Viet Nam claims in its first interim report that the administration in south Viet Nam has committed acts of terror in contravention of article 14(c) of the Geneva agreement.

1955   On 4 February the government of the Democratic Republic of Viet Nam calls for the restoration of normal relations between the two parts of Viet Nam.

On 28 February Saigon announces that elections will not be held in 1956.

On 6 April members of the International Control Commission are physically attacked by the Saigon authorities.

On 19 April agreement made between the Diem government and Michigan State University concerning the organisation and consolidation of police and security forces.

On 6 June the government of the Democratic Republic of Viet Nam calls for a conference to prepare elections.

On 8 July Diem's troops perpetrate a massacre in Huong Dien, Quang Tri province: 92 people killed, including 31 children and 32 women.

1955   On 16 July Diem declares that he does not consider himself bound by the Geneva agreement.

On 7 October the Diem government refuses to take part in talks in preparation for elections.

On 23 October Diem declares south Viet Nam to be the Republic of Viet Nam; the ex-emperor Bao Dai retires to the French Riviera.

On 27 November Diem's troops carry out a massacre in Cho Duoc.

According to incomplete reports, in the period July 1954 to December 1955 the Diem government committed about 4,584 terrorist acts in contravention of articles 14(c) and 15(d) of the Geneva agreement, with the following casualties: 2,042 killed or abducted, 4,555 wounded, 31,176 imprisoned and tortured.

On 29 December the Chief of the General Staff of the south Vietnamese government forces calls for the "liberation" of north Viet Nam.

1956   Ordinance 6 of the south Vietnamese government, published on 11 January, provides for custody in concentration camps of "people considered a danger to national defense and public safety."

On 20 March the campaign "Denounce the Communists" is launched; intensification of acts of terror against former resistance fighters and patriots.

On 28 April the French expeditionary force
withdraws.

PHASE VI

1956   On 8 May the co-chairmen of the Geneva
conference, Britain and the Soviet Union,
call on both governments in Viet Nam to
hold elections.
On 11 May the government of the Democratic Republic of Viet Nam requests Diem
again to start negotiations.
In June the "Temporary Equipment Recovery
Mission," consisting of 480 officers, is set up
in Saigon in contravention of the Geneva
agreement; followed by regular deliveries of
American war material.

1957   On 13 May Diem declares in New York,
"The borders of the United States extend to
the seventeenth parallel."
On 18 July the government of the Democratic Republic of Viet Nam sends yet another
note to the Diem government calling for
talks on elections; the "Service de Liaison
du Palais de la Présidence" is founded in Saigon and starts sabotage operations against
the DRV.

1958   In January the American airbase Ban Me
Thuot is constructed, together with other
strategic installations.
On 7 March the government of the DRV
proposes a meeting of delegates from both
parts of Viet Nam to discuss the resumption
of normal relations.
In March and April Diem's troops carry out
"cleaning up" operations in the provinces
Binh Dinh, Phu Yen, Binh Duong, Binh

Long, Bien Hoa and Tay Ninh.

On 20 September south Vietnamese troops carry out "cleaning up" operations in the provinces An Giang, An Xuyen, Ba Xuyen, Kien Giang, Phong Dinh and Vinh Long.

On 1 December a mass poisoning in the concentration camp of Phu Loi, where 6,000 political prisoners are interned, leads to the death of more than 1,000 prisoners; those seeking help are shot; subsequent "pacifying action" against the people in this area under the command of William Samuel, head of the Military Assistance Advisory Group (MAAG).

In December and the following January "cleaning up" operations in the provinces Ha Thien and Rach Gia, with more than 100 American advisers taking part.

In December the people of south Viet Nam begin their armed conflict against the Diem government.

1959 In April Diem declares south Viet Nam in a state of war.

In May "cleaning up" operation in the province Quang Ngai.

PHASE VII

1959 On 6 May the Law 10/59 comes into force, dealing with the setting up of courts-martial.

In July the number of American advisers rises from 200 to 2,000.

On 7 July Diem defines the creation of "welfare zones" as the main task of the year.

In August Da Nang is developed as provisioning base of the American navy.

In August and September "cleaning up" operations in the areas Ca Mau, Can Tho, Bac Lieu, Rach Gia and Tra Vinh.

In September 46 airfields are in use in south Viet Nam (compared with six in 1954), as well as 11 naval bases.

1960   In March "cleaning up" operations in the eastern regions of the provinces Quang Tri, Thua Thien and Quang Nam.

In July improvements carried out on the strategic roads from Dong Ha (south Viet Nam) to Tchepone (Laos) and from Dakto (south Viet Nam) to Attopeu (Laos).

PHASE VIII

1960   By December the number of American advisers has risen from 2,000 to 3,000; the number of American bases has risen to 57; according to incomplete records, casualties in the period July 1954 to December 1960 comprise about 527,000 people imprisoned and tortured and a further 77,500 killed.

On 20 December the National Front for the Liberation of South Viet Nam is founded.

1961   In February and March "cleaning up" operations in Ben Tre, Quang Nam, Phu Yen, Thu Dau Mot, My Tho and Dong Thap Muoi.

On 7 May meeting of the American National Security Council to discuss an extension of American aid and the commitment of American regular soldiers.

On 11 May Vice-President Lyndon B. Johnson visits south Viet Nam; a communiqué at the end of the visit signals the start of the

American "special war."

On 19 June a commission under Professor Eugene Staley visits Viet Nam; the Staley Plan worked out, aimed at a "pacification" of south Viet Nam within eighteen months.

On 2 July ten saboteurs arrested after air landings in the commune To Hieu in north Viet Nam.

On 18 October General Maxwell Taylor investigates in south Viet Nam the possibility of using American troops; the Staley-Taylor Plan worked out.

PHASE IX

1961 On 14 December President Kennedy assures Diem of full American support.

1962 On 10 January Diem announces that his government has worked out with the United States an experimental programme for the use of toxic chemicals.

On 4 February 60 officers and men of the U.S. Air Force take a direct part in an attack on the inhabitants of the area An Xuyen in the Mekong delta.

On 8 February the Military Assistance Command, Viet Nam (MACV) under General Harkins takes over the supervision of military operations in south Viet Nam.

PHASE X

1962 On 22 March the operation "Sunrise" is launched in the battle area of the Thu Da Mot province under the command of Colo-

nels William N. Osborne and Carl Schaad.
In April 500 "Special Forces" arrive from
Fort Bragg, North Carolina.

By December there are 11,000 American
soldiers in south Viet Nam; 27,000 "cleaning
up" operations and 50,000 air sorties carried
out.

1963 On 2 January battle near Ap Bac; armed
forces of the National Liberation Front score
a victory against south Vietnamese and
American troops.

On 8 February General Harkins declares,
"Viet Nam has become for the American
troops a practice ground for anti-guerrilla
tactics."

On 13 April a sabotage squad is taken prisoner in the commune Kien Thanh in north
Viet Nam.

On 8 May first major clashes between Bud-
dhists and south Vietnamese government
troops in Hue.

On 4 June a sabotage squad taken prisoner
in the region of Yen Tu, north Viet Nam.

On 11 June the first Buddhist monk sets fire
to himself in protest against government oppression.

On 16 July a sabotage squad taken prisoner
in the district of Mong Cay, north Viet Nam.

On 1 November Ngo Dinh Diem and Ngo
Dinh Nhu murdered; government dismissed
by General Duong Van Minh.

1964 On 9 March the Rostow Plan No. 6 becomes
known, envisaging the extension of the war
to the Democratic Republic of Viet Nam.

On 14 May Secretary of Defense McNamara
declares, "The United States does not ex-
clude the possibility of carrying the war into

north Viet Nam."

By June the United States has 169 airfields and 11 naval bases in south Viet Nam.

On 30 July American ships enter north Vietnamese territorial waters and shell the islands Hen Ngu, 2½ miles from the coast, and Hon Me, 7½ miles from the coast.

On 1 August American planes bomb the frontier post Nam Can, 4 miles from the Viet Nam–Laos border, and the village of Moong De, 12 miles from the border.

On 2 August seven American planes bomb the frontier post again; exchange of fire between the American destroyer *Maddox* and north Vietnamese torpedo-boats in the Bay of Tonking inside the 12-mile limit.

On 3 August American warships shell the region of Ron and Deo Ngang in the Quang Binh province.

On 4 August President Johnson declares that north Viet Nam is guilty of an act of provocation against American ships in the Bay of Tonking.

On 5 August President Johnson calls on Congress for full authority to carry out "all necessary steps to protect our forces and to support the states inside SEATO"; both houses of Congress grant the authority by 504 votes to 2 (Senators Morse and Gruening).

First "act of reprisal" by the Seventh Fleet on targets within the Democratic Republic of Viet Nam.

PETER WEISS

Peter Weiss was born at Nowawes, near Berlin, but left Germany when Nazism came in. He has lived in Sweden ever since, although he continues to write in German. In addition to the plays that established his worldwide fame, he has written novels and made experimental films.

LEE BAXANDALL

Lee Baxandall, who translated Song of the Lusitanian Bogey, *has also translated plays by Bertolt Brecht, and his own plays have been acted at La Mama and elsewhere. He was an editor of the pioneering theoretical journal of the New Left,* Studies on the Left, *and has published articles in many other journals.*

GEOFFREY SKELTON

Geoffrey Skelton, translator of Discourse on . . . Viet Nam, *was born in South Africa of British parents and educated in England. After World War II he spent seven years in Germany with the Foreign Office information service, followed by ten years with the German Service of the British Broadcasting Corporation. His book* Wagner at Bayreuth *was published in 1966, and his many translations include Peter Weiss's* Marat/Sade, *for which he and Adrian Mitchell were awarded the P.E.N. translation prize in the United States.*